Northern Wildflower

a memoir

CATHERINE LAFFERTY

Roseway Publishing
an imprint of Fernwood Publishing
HALIFAX & WINNIPEG

Editing: Leanne Betasamosake Simpson and Fazeela Jiwa
Cover beadwork: Norine Lafferty
Design: Tania Craan
Printed and bound in Canada

Published by Roseway Publishing
an imprint of Fernwood Publishing
32 Oceanvista Lane, Black Point, Nova Scotia, B0J 1B0
and 748 Broadway Avenue, Winnipeg, Manitoba, R3G 0X3
www.fernwoodpublishing.ca/roseway

Fernwood Publishing Company Limited gratefully acknowledges the financial support of the Government of Canada through the Canada Book Fund, the Canada Council for the Arts, Arts Nova Scotia, the Province of Nova Scotia and the Province of Manitoba for our publishing program.

Library and Archives Canada Cataloguing in Publication

Lafferty, Catherine, 1982-, author
Northern wildflower / Catherine Lafferty.

Issued in print and electronic formats.
ISBN 978-1-77363-040-3 (softcover).--ISBN 978-1-77363-041-0 (EPUB).--
ISBN 978-1-77363-042-7 (Kindle)

1. Lafferty, Catherine, 1982-. 2. Chipewyan Indians--Canada--Biography. 3. Indian women--Canada--Biography. I. Title.

E99.C59L34 2018   971.004'972   C2018-903704-0
                                      C2018-904496-9

To My Grandma

Acknowledgements

THIS BOOK WOULDN'T BE POSSIBLE without the help of many amazing, supportive and loving people that I have crossed paths with along my journey.

First, I would like to thank my children for being my most fierce critics and making sure that I don't take things too seriously.

I'd like to thank my friends and extended family for supporting me in my writing journey and providing me with honest advice because that is what family and friends do best.

I'd like to thank my mentors Richard Van Camp and Leanne Betasamosake Simpson for being motivating, generous guiding lights. I am grateful for their valuable insight and the time they set aside for me.

To everyone in my life that has taught me to be strong, without life's tough lessons I wouldn't be the person I am today. Thank you for adding another layer of depth to my life and bringing out the bravery in me.

I'd like to thank my mom for always being patient with me, showing kindness and unconditional love.

I'd like to thank my grandparents for giving me everything I ever needed. They gave me just the right amounts of love, discipline, freedom and lifelong values and beliefs that I will forever stand for. I look forward to seeing you again.

MAHSI CHO!

*This book was written in hopes of inspiring,
encouraging and giving hope to
the Indigenous Peoples of Canada that are in the struggle.
Together we can break the cycle of intergenerational trauma
and echo our voices loud and clear, in unity and solidarity,
so that every person will understand the
detrimental effects that colonialism has had
on our livelihood throughout Canada's history.*

Foreword

BY LEANNE BETASAMOSAKE SIMPSON

I FIRST MET CATHERINE AT Dechinta Centre for Research and Learning — a Dene Bush University in Denedeh. Catherine was at one of our on-the-land gatherings as a councillor from the Yellowknives Dene First Nation. At the time, our programming was operating in the Akaitcho region of Denendeh on Chief DryGeese Territory — Catherine's homeland. Catherine was there as a community leader, with her two gorgeous children, who immediately connected with my own kids. The group of them had a wonderful time over the next few days fishing nets, swimming, making dry fish and just being Indigenous kids. Together. At the time, I didn't know Catherine was also a writer.

A few years later, Catherine emailed me to ask for help with a book-length memoir project she was working on. It has been rare in my life that young writers approach me with fully completed manuscripts, particularly Indigenous writers that have completed such enormous projects in relative isolation, with little support and encouragement from a writing community or any community for that matter. This has, however, been the beautiful struggle of generations of Indigenous writers, particularly Indigenous women. Catherine's work immediately reminded me of Maria Campbell's *Halfbreed*, Lee Maracle's *I am Woman* and the poetry of Joanne Arnott. Even more importantly, it reminded me of Dene storytellers and the act of telling one's own story as a practice of affirming our experiences, connecting to the ones that have come before us and our homelands and speaking our own truths on our own terms. *Northern Wildflower* also serves as a counterpoint to the academic work of Dene scholar Glen Coulthard because it represents a very personal, intimate exploration of the themes of dispossession, violence, disconnection and resistance from the perspective of a young Dene woman.

Often, in teaching in the North, I find it difficult to find relevant readings for my Dene students. I am excited to share Catherine's book with them, because I know they will, perhaps for the first time, see their lives and their experiences in print. This was reinforced for me this year at Yellowknife's writers' festival, NorthWords. Catherine read an excerpt of her book to a packed room in the basement of the Yellowknife Centre on a panel with myself, Paul Andrew, Tracey Lindberg and Rosanna Deerchild — a pretty intimidating panel for an emerging Indigenous writer. Catherine read after Elder Paul Andrew spoke of his residential school experience and the strength and resilience of the Shuhtaotine or Mountain Dene. Her reading was powerful and moving, holding the audience in silence as she told her story. Her community connected with the work and that was wonderful to witness.

Memoir is not an easy genre, particularly for Indigenous women. We rarely get the opportunity to tell our stories, and when we do, we are often met with racism, patriarchy and judgement. I can't think of any other young Dene women who have written memoirs, and that makes this story all the more important. From an artistic standpoint, it can be difficult to tell the story of our lives to audiences that may not fully understand the colonial context that is responsible for the violence in our lives. I think Catherine does an excellent job of truth telling while not succumbing to a victim narrative.

Northern Wildflower is a beautiful story of Dene resistance. It is a call for a just world, and it will inspire a new generation of young Dene writers and storytellers to speak up, to write and to live their very best lives.

— *Leanne Betasamosake Simpson*

Chapter 1

*E*VERYONE HAS A UNIQUE STORY TO TELL. This is mine. Memories strung together like beads, sewn onto smoked moose hide in the shape of a northern wildflower drawn by my grandmother.

My journey began on Easter Sunday in the early eighties. My parents were at a drive-through theatre in a small northern Alberta oil town when I made my debut into this world.

I proved to be fiery from the start. I had light red hair and eyebrows that would turn bright red when I cried; I was born with a passion that I couldn't hide. I get my auburn traits from my dad, a freckle-faced redhead from the east coast. I get my brazen personality from my mother, a black-haired beauty one generation away from being born in a teepee.

I cried nights on end while they walked the floors with me in their small apartment. My mom often reminds me that no one ever wanted to babysit me because I cried too much. I was colicky and inconsolable.

My mom would rock me in my homemade Dene swing made from a sheet, some rope and two sticks, which hung from one corner of the ceiling above her bed to the other. A Dene invention was the only thing that would help me fall asleep — no wonder I like hammocks so much.

It's safe to say that I was a restless child from my entrance into this world, and I've carried this feeling of yearning in my heart throughout my life.

I have a constant irritation with the status quo and am rarely satisfied. I always want more. Not in the sense of material things but in the sense of wanting a better world, a just world, especially for those who grew up like me, knowing what it's like to live as an outsider on your own territory. Knowing what it feels like to grow up in a system that doesn't accept you, the same system that forced you to be dependent on it.

I want there to be a better world for Indigenous people who have felt what it's like to live in a society that has already developed a preconceived notion that we are failures, that we have a meek future, that we will end up drunk like the parents that couldn't raise us, that we will end up abusing the system with our countless needs of taxpayer dollars, that we are not worthy to eat at the big table, that we should be thankful and consider ourselves lucky enough to live off the crumbs they give us. There has got to be something better for those who know what it's like to feel hopeless and disingenuously pitied by those who watch us fall through the cracks because they believe there's no hope for us. We aren't even considered human, after all. The worst part is that some Indigenous people also have this perception of themselves and where they come from because they have lost their cultural identities through social conditioning efforts.

I want justice. I want to take back our stolen identities. Our pride has been ripped and torn to shreds from the years of deliberate trauma that was served to us in the form of righteous, all-knowing authority. The wicked rules that have been written in a heavy ink are made to look like they can't be erased, but those rules can be broken, those policies can be amended, those laws can be overturned and those words that hold us down can be burned.

I want our men to be warriors again and our women to be safe and respected. I want our land back, our homes back, our families back, our health back. We were forced to detach from everything we knew right down to the very core of who we are. I want things back to the way they once were. The Dene once lived in harmony without interruption and influence, and that worked well for us. I won't be fully satisfied until I see the day that we are no longer told to do things any other way but the way we know, our way.

I won't be content until the day that I feel like I belong on my own soil. Until the day that I don't have to work twice as hard to get that management job even though I have a higher education. Until the day that I don't walk past the post office and see my relatives on the street being ridiculed and stereotyped for being intoxicated and homeless. Until the day I never hear another Indian joke. Until the day that I don't have to worry that my son will end up in jail because he was profiled and discriminated against. Until the day that I don't have to worry that my daughter will be abused because she's considered worthless in the eyes of those who feel they are superior to her. Until the day I don't have to argue with someone when I hear them say, "Why can't you just get over it?" Until the day that everyone understands why we won't get over it.

Until then, I will not rest. I will keep fighting the good fight to make sure I see a change in this world, until the silenced voices can speak again. Until we can make our own rules and until we can be sure that no one takes advantage of us anymore. I didn't know these injustices existed when I was brought into this world, but I could feel them through my mother's womb and as time went on I inevitably encountered them in my everyday life.

My family grew up constantly struggling on our own land when we should have been treated like royalty, with the respect and dignity we deserved. Instead, we were forced to assimilate, often violently. Our minds, bodies and self-determination were not and are still not respected to this day. Our vision of our treaty is continually erased, and we are always having to stand up for our rights even in the most mundane circumstances. It's tiring.

I don't think our people ever realized the full extent of how the future for them would unravel. No one except the Elders could have predicted the impacts that would send a generational ripple of devastation throughout Canada. The Elders always talk about how money encroached upon their livelihood. The few Elders that are still alive today witnessed first-hand how our people slowly started to become more and more reliant on it. Money eventually became too powerful of a force to stop. "Money doesn't grow on trees," my mom would say, and I would say, "Yes it does, it's made of paper." It took me a long time to realize that money was earned through working for other people and not for ourselves.

In the olden days, when our people worked they worked with their hands on the land because it was the only way to survive. They worked hard for their food and shelter and they enjoyed it. There was no such thing as being idle. Then, something happened when money crept into the North. Our people did not fit into the new working world because they had little to no formal education, and they weren't readily accepted into the mould that was determined fitting enough to obtain the jobs that were created when the government and the mining industries welcomed themselves in. The North became a rewarding scene for southerners seeking adventure, new beginnings and prosperity. This left little room for the Dene, who did not require those things to be happy, and almost overnight the Dene way of living almost disappeared through the exclusiveness of those who celebrate money.

As a child, I couldn't grasp the concept or the importance of money and how it was something that people strived to obtain all their lives. As an adult, I still don't understand why most of us spend our lives racing to get to the top, breaking our backs in the process and struggling to make ends meet only to end up counting down until retirement.

There has got to be more to life. I want a deeper fulfillment. I want my soul to be full of purpose and substance. I don't want to drag myself out of bed every morning cringing at the thought of the work week ahead of me. I want to jump up out of bed every morning knowing that I am doing what I love without restriction, without worrying about money.

Unfortunately, until that day comes, money makes the world go around and enriches our lives with a false sense of happiness, materialism and security. Maybe I have come to think that it shouldn't have to be this way because of my humble beginnings.

My first memories are of my parents throwing small parties in our tiny concrete basement suite just outside of Toronto, a skip and a hop away from the busiest highway in North America. I could see them from the crack in my bedroom door, laughing and dancing in the middle of the night and listening to country music long after I had been sent to bed. But I was a night owl and tried to stay up just as late as they did. I could barely see them with my vision a blur, so I would squint hard just to see the outline of their figures — I had bad eyes, but my mom didn't know I needed glasses yet.

During the day, my dad would go to work building houses while my mom and I curled up on the couch together and watched game shows as I ruffled her hair. I've always been fascinated with hair and used to pretend I was a hairdresser. My best friend Sarah lived across the street from me and she would come over to play. Sarah and I decided to play hairdresser one

*Catherine with a juice stained mouth
and pearl hoop earrings
(photo credit Norine Lafferty)*

day before class pictures. I was the hairdresser and she was the client. My grandma happened to be visiting us and I snitched her sewing scissors from the kitchen table. Sarah and I hid in the bathroom until my mom noticed that we were too quiet. "Catherine, you open this door right now!" She banged her fist on the locked bathroom door, insisting that I open it. I reassured her that I would just be a few more minutes, but I knew I was in trouble. When Sarah came out of the bathroom, her once-beautiful, long, strawberry-blonde hair was snipped short and stuck flat to her head with a few spikes sticking up here and there. I still have her school picture tucked away somewhere, reminding me that hairdressing is not my calling.

In those days, I used to play with two brothers, Robby and Billy. Our moms were best friends, so they would often come over to visit us. One day Robby accidently ripped one of the little golden hoop pearl earrings right out of my ear while he was wrestling with me, and I screamed in pain. I had worn those earrings ever since I was a baby. My mom had brought me to get my pointy elf ears pierced for my baby pictures when I was just learning how to sit up by myself. She had seen a little girl from India who had her ears pierced and thought it looked cultural.

I wonder how my mother felt moving to such a big city

after living in a small northern town her entire life. I know she lived in fear of losing me when we were out in public, so she would part my hair down the middle and braid both sides, then tie a little bell at the bottom of each braid so she could hear me running around the grocery store if I wandered too far. So, it's safe to say she almost suffered a heart attack when I didn't listen after she told me to hold onto her pant leg while she was in line at a food truck vendor at an outdoor country music concert with over one hundred thousand people. My parents searched for almost an hour and had people join the search, yelling out my name on the lookout for a little Dene girl with ornamental braids, until my dad found me crying at the front of the stage near the fenced-off area. I remember looking up to see his shadow hovering over me, half angry and half relieved.

My parents were very young when they had me. They weren't ready for a baby. My dad was a carpenter by trade, and he grew up in a large family. His dad, who was also a carpenter, died in a work accident when my dad was just a baby. My dad was left to help his mother look after the family and he worked hard his whole life, from a young age.

My parents met at a bonfire party in northern Alberta. They were both there for the oil boom. My mom moved from her small hometown of Yellowknife, Northwest Territories, as soon as she was old enough to get out on her own and move in with her older sister Clara. My mom said she saw my dad from across the fire and thought he was cute, so she got his attention by throwing rocks at him; that must be where I get my terrible flirting skills from.

They only lasted a few years together after I came into the picture. One day, without any warning, my mom packed up what belongings we had in our little basement apartment and left my dad with nothing but a broken heart. I still remember

Catherine and her Dad playing cards (photo credit Norine Lafferty)

the image of my dad the day we left and the broken look in his eyes when we said our goodbyes. When I look back now, I can see him sitting in our dark and empty basement suite crying with his head in his hands. I hugged him one last time while my mom waited for me at the top of the stairs, the same stairs where he taught me how to tie my shoes and figure out my left foot from my right, essential skills I needed to know for my first day of kindergarten.

I sometimes wonder where I would be today if we had stayed, but I can't think that way because I can't go back to that time and change it. Even if I could change the past, I'm not sure that I would. The journey I have travelled may have led me down dark paths a time or two, but I believe I am where I'm supposed to be. Life is an intricate, winding road that leads us through good times and bad. We never know what might happen from one minute to the next, but I believe that if we have faith our paths will eventually lead us to where we are supposed to be.

I didn't think I would ever see my dad again. We had completely lost contact. Our nightly routine of "I love you more than the whole wide world" and "I love you more than the universe" would never be spoken again, but those are the keepsakes that I store away in my memory of the father I knew once upon a time.

❧

MY MOM, HER NEW BOYFRIEND and I travelled across Canada in his beat-up camper van. Little did I know then that the stranger I just met would be in my life more than my own father.

The highway was so foreign and magical to me. I enjoyed the scenery in between sleeping, gassing up at truck stops along the way and prying open red pistachios until my fingers were stained blood red.

We set up camp in southern Alberta, which is where we would live for the next few years of our lives until my mother and stepdad would go their separate ways (only to reconcile a few years later).

My memories of living in Calgary were pleasant, for the most part. I would bike up and down the hill behind my house that had a perfect view of the Saddledome. I was always out biking. I could bike with no hands, showing off to myself for hours. Sure, I crashed on my bike all the time and would come home bruised and scraped, but I loved it. Cruising down hills at full speed gave me a sense of invincibility and freedom. Freedom was something that ranked high on my priority list from an early age. I somehow knew that, without freedom, I would not be able to live — I wouldn't be able to be me.

I loved cruising on the smooth black pavement in the middle of the road with the wind in my hair and my hands stretched out as if I was hugging the air, not worrying about what was in front of me. I was fearless and naïve, a deadly combination.

The worst crash I can remember was when I was biking home from the corner store with a plastic bag full of junk food hanging from my handle bars. It got caught in the spokes and I flew off the bike head first, doing a flip in the air. I had landed on the curb of the sidewalk and was giving myself some time to check my wounds when a man pulled up beside me in an old car. He rolled down the window and said, "Hi, do you need some help?"

I quickly jumped back on my bike and said, "No thanks, I'm fine," and kept my head down as I peddled home as fast as I could. "It's okay, I know your mom, I know where you live," he said as he stepped on the gas to keep up with my momentum. All I could imagine was him throwing me in the trunk of his car and speeding away, leaving only my bike as a small clue as to what happened if I went missing. When I got home he was at my house and it turns out he was, in fact, a friend of my mom's. I could tell she was pleased with me, though, that I knew better than to get into a car with a total stranger by the look she gave me out of the corner of her eye.

We weren't in Calgary long enough for me to make any lasting friends. I invited some of the girls in my class to my birthday party and only one friend showed up. I tried to act like I didn't care, but deep down I felt like no one liked me. I desperately wanted to make friends and not feel like an outsider, but I wasn't in one place long enough to feel like I had a place I could call home. My sense of home was where we set up camp until we migrated again. Since I had been a baby I had been shuffled around and, eventually, certain places had less and less significance for me. Home became wherever I lay my head to rest.

Chapter 2

 $\mathcal{M}$ Y MOM AND I FOUND OURSELVES back in her northern hometown of Yellowknife and living temporarily in my grandmother's one-bedroom apartment after she broke things off with my stepdad. She would often leave me with my grandma to frequent the infamous Gold Range bar.

The Gold Range is a renowned hotel and bar smack dab in the centre of downtown Yellowknife. It's a rowdy, loud, gritty bar with an old tavern atmosphere. Built in the golden age, it's one of the oldest buildings still standing in Yellowknife. When you walk into the "Strange Range" you feel like you are transported back in time. Regulars line up along the walls and at the bar staring at all the newcomers walking in. There's always an unmistakably strong scent of rancid beer and whisky in the air and an old band that plays the honkytonk blues enticing patrons to get up and dance to show off their two step.

With my grandma, I felt safe. My grandparents lived a quiet life. My grandparents never lived together; they lived in the same apartment building but had separate units. My grandma lived on the fourth floor and my papa lived directly under her three floors down. She could only put up with my papa for so long until she got annoyed. This went on to the point that they wouldn't talk for weeks, sometimes months, until eventually they would start again right back where they left off. Living under different roofs must have been what made it work for them.

Before she moved to Yellowknife, my grandma grew up on an island off the North Shore of the Great Slave Lake, where the winters were unforgiving. She lived solely off the land with no running water or electricity. Her father was a trapper. As far as I know, her great grandfather came to the North from Europe with his three brothers and they spread the family tree far and wide throughout the North. Although written records weren't readily kept back then, my ancestors passed down this information orally and, to this day, when I introduce myself to the Elders I tell them who my grandparents are so they will know which family line I come from.

One thing I do know is that I have a lot of cousins. I don't even know most of them. I invited a few of my cousins over for Christmas dinner one year and my house turned into a surprise family reunion. An important law in our culture is to share what we have, so when we have a get together we usually have a large feast and invite everyone we know. We also never turn down an offering especially when it comes to food.

Word got around the community that I was having people over and about thirty hungry relatives showed up to my tiny trailer. I had an assembly line set up in my kitchen that led all the way to the back of the house. My mom had to get on my daughter's karaoke machine to shout, "Dinner's ready!" over all the noise. I had to open the door in minus forty to let out some heat out because the place was steaming up and the turkey was burning. My mom and I didn't know half of our cousin's names and we felt guilty because we should have; after all, we were one big family.

There were little runny-nosed kids with juice stains around their mouths snooping around my bedroom and going through my things. I didn't mind because I was once a juice-stained, runny-nosed kid too. Looking at my childhood photos, there is not one picture of me that does not have a ring of pink or yellow juice stained across the top of my mouth. My grandma always made sure there was plenty of juice in the fridge for me.

My grandma's grandmother was full Slavey but she was registered as a Dogrib. I used to think that the Dogrib people travelled North by dog team thousands of years ago, and the people got so cold they ended up having to eat their own dogs to survive, which is why they were named Dog Ribs. But the word Dogrib comes from the word "Tłįchǫ." The legend has it that the Tłįchǫ descended from a dog-like human, a shape-shifter.

There are many stories of shape-shifters in the North and most of them are unpleasant. They are what we call the bushman or the Nàhga. There have been accounts of people seeing the Nàhga in the North, usually along the highways between the smaller northern communities. The one that scares me the most is the story of a woman that is dressed in old clothes from the 1950s and hitchhiking on the side of the road. When people look at her closely, they can see that she is half woman and half caribou because she has hooves for feet. Most Elders will tell you not to talk about these things if they don't concern you — they are considered unmentionable.

Shape-shifters or not, you have got to be tough to survive the harsh cold winters in the North, especially in the days before running water and electricity, so I pride myself on the strong ancestral bloodline that I come from. The winters in the North can be deadly. When the temperature drops to minus fifty and metal is so cold that it turns hot, that's when you know to stay indoors. I can't help but wonder if the cold preserves me or if it just ages me quicker when I'm overexposed to it, which I often am because I don't tend to dress for the weather.

The tourists love the cold, though, and embrace it like

children as they bundle up and make snow angels on the ice road. I wonder what they think, flying over the lake and seeing a vast territory of ice and rock in the middle of nowhere. It's a land that is seen by outsiders as the Great White North, the last frontier. What they don't see is a land that is full and rich with a brilliant history of ancient legends, endless trap lines, hunting grounds and sacred sites.

I try to see my home from a fresh perspective every time I come back to it from somewhere else and look at it through a new lens, from a tourist's eyes. Wondering if it's as spectacular as everyone says it is after all. Maybe I have just not seen it from that viewpoint because I often feel isolated in it. I love my home, though. It is the only place that I feel like I belong, and I miss it when I am gone for too long. It's the water, the wind, the sky, my family and friends. It's all of it intertwined, and it always calls me home.

My ancestors trapped, fished and hunted because they had to. Sadly, many of my relatives today wouldn't know how to live off the land. Most of us have lost our ability to practise our traditions because efforts of assimilation have urbanized many of us.

I will be the first to tell you that if I were ever lost in the bush I would probably not survive in the elements alone. I can't chop wood to start a fire to keep me warm or build a shelter. This is not something I'm proud of. However, I am actively introducing myself and my children to our Dene cultural practices, and together we are learning how to live on the land by reclaiming a piece of our territory and building a home for ourselves. We are starting by simply putting up a canvas tent with a wood stove and a spruce-bough floor to keep us warm. I am fortunate to be able to pass on my Dene teachings to my children through other avenues as well. I do this through my commitment to my community and through my ability to nurture and guide my children to be good people. As a mother, I try to embody the practice of my Dene traditions through the love and care of my children, and I try to live up to the Dene laws by teaching them through my actions. But things weren't always this way.

I am one of the many Dene of my age who has been deprived of being able to immerse myself in my culture. A large part of our identity has been lost because it was once stolen, but we are slowly trying to gain it back through occupying ourselves with the teachings of the Elders and through drawing forth our genetic memories to bring our traditions out from our sleeping senses.

One of the teachings I learned from my grandma early on was to never take advantage of the land. My grandma instilled a fear in me to never be too confident when out on the water, and because of this I never fully embark on an adventure without some hesitancy. She was right to scare me, because there have been many times when I wished I had listened to her but learned the hard way instead when I found myself in dangerous situations. This is the reason I am overly cautious when I travel, and everywhere I go I try to remember to drop a coin on the ground, throw some tobacco in the water, carry a piece of rat root medicine with me to ward off evil spirits and give thanks for my safe travels, like I was taught.

A long list of beliefs passed down to me includes never leaving a drawer open for worry that it is an invite for unexpected guests, from both this world and the spirit world. I was also taught that if you party too much in your home, you will be visited by all sorts of spirits. These spirits can wreak havoc on your home if they are negative, and they most often are when alcohol is abused. They can cause your pipes to freeze up, your furnace to give out and your appliances to malfunction, similar to a poltergeist.

Catherine, her Kookum, her Grandma and mother — 4 Generations

Kookum

I hope to live as long as my great grandma did. My Kookum lived until she was over one hundred years old, but no one knows for sure how old she was because, somewhere along the way, she stopped counting. I call her my Kookum instead of my Ehtsi because of the Cree in me from my papa's side.

I only have a faint memory of my Kookum, but I cherish it greatly. It is one of my first memories. The simple act of helping her lift her teacup to her mouth is ingrained in my mind. Her tea was spilling over because of her trembling hands, so I held it steady for her and she held my hand in hers, thanking me with her eyes. Her hands were so wrinkly and bony but as soft as silk where they were once tough and strong from a life of hard work out on the land. I can still see the fine details of the flowers on the teacup and the deep lines in her skin, which represented her wisdom. Her eyes were full of familiarity and held so much knowledge; they told a story of their own. I hope I never lose that memory of her and the timeless moment we shared.

Some say my Kookum was a medicine woman. My Kookum is the one who passed her beliefs down to my grandma. In her day, there was powerful medicine. My Kookum would not let anyone near her hair and, at the end of her life, she had a large ball of it tucked away so that no one could use bad medicine on her or use it for bad medicine on others.

*

MY GRANDMA AND PAPA WERE never married, which was very progressive at the time. Together, they had six children. Three boys and three girls. My grandma was as tough as a buffalo; she had a steadfast heart. One minute she would be chasing me and my friends down the hallway with a straw broom, and the next minute she would serve me up some hotcakes and chocolate milk.

You could never catch my grandma wearing pants, or slacks as she would call them. She only wore pleated skirts and flower-print dresses. If she was

Papa & Grandma

Old Fort Rae, view of the lake
(photo credit Catherine Lafferty)

going out on the town, she would don a silk flower-print scarf on her head to keep the wind out of her ears when she went outside. It's a fashion that most of the Dene Elders wear in the North. In fact, most Dene grandmas dress the same. They all wear colourful printed scarfs over their ears, purple or blue windbreaker jackets, dark tights, white socks and black ankle boots lined with fur at the top. Whenever I would go down south, my grandma would ask me to look through thrift stores for pleated skirts and queen-sized, spice-coloured tights, and to this day I still keep an eye out for her fashions.

My grandma's father spoke French and her mother only spoke in her native tongue, yet they had sixteen children together. My grandma was a twin, but her twin sister died of sickness as a baby. They were born on the island of Old Fort Rae in the fall of 1925. Old Fort Rae is on the North Arm of the Great Slave Lake and is about an hour and a half boat ride from Behchoko and another hour drive to Yellowknife. It is where my grandma would spend her childhood, and she never left the island until she was a teenager.

Old Fort Rae, rhubarb patch
(photo credit Catherine Lafferty)

Old Fort Rae is a perfectly round island when viewed from above, and archeological studies have shown that it is an odd land formation. Now a historical site, it is where one of the first trading posts was established in the North. When I was a teenager I used to visit Old Fort Rae by boat for our large family gatherings in the summer. The boat ride over was always frightening. The waves would be so high that when the boat crashed down on them, I thought it would snap in half.

There are fields of fresh rhubarb, onions and berries that now grow wild in Old Fort Rae, planted there during the fur

Old Fort Rae, gazebo and cross
(photo credit Catherine Lafferty)

trade. My cousins and I would four-wheel our way through the tall bushes in the hot summer sun, most likely trampling over historical artifacts but not knowing that we were being so reckless.

My grandma would tell me not to run in the fields at night because that is when the spirits roam, and I could swear I seen one of them one night, dressed in white and slowly walking behind one of the canvas tents.

Once, my grandma pointed out a small island with a pine tree on it that you could faintly see from the top of the hill with the naked eye. It looked like a man being pulled by a dog team. She told me that, when she was younger, she would look out at the frozen lake and sometimes think that it was her dad on his dog team coming home from his trap line. "Grandma did you miss him when he went away?" I would ask her, and she would say, with pride, "Yes, he was a good father to me." She told me how she would often worry about him when he was gone for long periods of time.

When the missionaries came to get her and her siblings,

my grandma was forced to leave the island as a child. They were taken from the only home they knew to sit in a classroom and learn a new language, proper manners and how to pray, something that the nuns didn't believe that the Dene people had already established for themselves in their own way.

My grandma was one of the many Indigenous children to be taken away from her family to learn how to be a "civilized" member of society. She seldom discussed what happened to her during her stay in the residential school, but she did share the experience of having to eat rotten fish and getting her hair cut short after the nuns had forcefully dunked her head in a barrel of coal oil because she was considered "unclean."

She was spared from having to spend more than a year at the residential school. When she returned for the summer from her first year at school, she told her parents what happened to her there and asked her dad not to let them take her again in the fall. Since she was the eldest of her siblings, she was needed around the house to help her mother care for the younger ones while her father was out trapping, and it was for that reason alone that she was able to stay. When the missionaries came back later that summer to collect the children, her father met them at the shoreline when they pulled up in their canoes. He made the case that she couldn't go, and they reluctantly agreed. Surprisingly, he was neither arrested, nor did they have to flee from their home like so many other Indigenous families had to do to spare their children.

When going through my grandma's keepsakes, I came across an old photo of a place that looked like the residential school. I was too young to understand the weight of it all, but the picture told me something wasn't right. It was in an old, rustic yellow colour and there were many children in the picture along the shoreline of the lake. Some were gathering wood; some were hauling water, but they all were in uniform and had the same sad look on their face. The nuns were also in the picture, but something was different about them. They were all looking directly at the camera with a serious look on their face. When I took a closer look it almost looked like they were floating, like they didn't belong in the picture at all. I had to squint to make out their feet, but only saw the ground where their feet should have been. I ran and showed the picture to my grandma, and she just shook her head in silence. I don't know what ever happened to that picture, but it was a very haunting glimpse into the shameful legacy that the residential schools left behind.

My grandma never did fully learn to read or write, but in her only year of residential school my grandma learned how to print her name so meticulously that, in her later years, she would take the time to write her full name including her middle name, Augustine, which I proudly share with her. Her signature usually took a full five minutes to pen out and she would always remind people of where she learned how to handwrite because it was the only learning lesson that she decided to take with her from her time at school. She could speak six different languages: Slavey, Chipewyan, Cree, Tłįchǫ, English and French, and the missionaries were never able to take her language away from her. She especially knew how to swear at me in Tłįchǫ when she was mad. I never did learn how to speak my language. Both Tłįchǫ and English were spoken equally in my home and I leaned more toward English because of the school system, but I knew what a swear word sounded like when I did something to upset her. For a long time, I did not understand why my grandma did not take the time to teach me our language. I don't think my grandma realized how precious our language was and that it would one day be so highly regarded or that it would need to be saved. She would have probably taken more time to teach me if she knew that our Indigenous languages would be considered one of the most significant, valuable resources we have as Indigenous people. This is why we need to work diligently on reclaiming our languages through our stories and songs.

My grandma would love to tell me stories of her younger years. She would tell me proudly of how she worked in the kitchen of the historic Wildcat Café for a dollar a day washing dishes and that a dollar a day was more than enough to get by in those days. But her time dishwashing was short

Catherine and her Grandma

lived. My grandmother was drawn to something else, something that was fulfilling for her. She was an expert seamstress by way of spending her time sewing with her mother while at home during the residential school era, and because most of her time was devoted to her craft she became the best at what she did. Sewing, like our language, is a large part of our culture; however, I don't ever remember picking up a needle and thread to bead. My grandma never did force anything on me. She would only encourage me if I showed interest in something, and sadly I did not show interest in sewing. Instead, I would rather roll tobacco for my papa with his old-fashioned cigarette roller while I listened to my grandma tell me stories of her younger days.

Her sewing was so sought after that she was asked to sew a beaded sash for the Pope. It was a project that made her beam with delight. She was humbly honoured. She loved the Pope. She was a religious woman but never went to church except for once a year for the Christmas Mass at midnight.

I realized how faithful my grandma was one day when she got stuck in the elevator on the fourth floor of our apartment building. I would race her up the stairs while she took the elevator and the one time I beat her to the top was when she got stuck. She was yelling at me through the elevator door, "Catherine, get the holy water on my nightstand!" I ran to get the holy water, her precious saving grace, and repeatedly splashed it on the doors while praying frantically for her freedom. Our faith must have been strong that day, because it worked.

Whenever we moved into a new house, my grandma would always make sure to have an old jam jar or spray bottle full of holy water that she would splash around the house to bless the place. Both of my grandparents were very spiritual. They shared many losses in their lifetime. As parents, they suffered the loss of three of their sons. I am only able to gather bits and pieces of what happened to my uncles, because my family found it too hard to talk about those painful memories.

When my grandparents met, my grandma moved off the island to the community of Fort Rae (Behchoko). My papa worked for the government. He was not from the area; in fact, his father was from North Dakota and moved to northern Alberta where he met my papa's mother, a Métis woman with Cree roots. My papa's parents owned the historic Rex Café in Yellowknife's Old Town, and my grandparents named their youngest son after it. Together, my grandparents had my aunt Clara, my mother, three boys, and my youngest auntie, Loretta, who came along when my grandma was later in life.

My mom took the loss of her youngest brother Rex the hardest; they were very close. To this day, my mom finds it hard to talk about Rex, and when I bring up his name, she turns her head to hide her tears and pretends to be busy doing something, anything, to not have to face the hurt. There is so much pain in our family from our losses, but I believe that talking about the hurt and the grief helps to heal us.

Through the years my grandma would hear reports of people seeing someone that looked like Rex in some small town along the Mexican border, or there would be reports of a body turned up somewhere and she would have to go through the process of providing blood samples and statements all over again. My grandma eventually grew weary of the rumours and the hopeless leads. She refused to believe that her son would have run away from his family never to be heard from again, and after a while, my grandma just wanted to be left alone.

It was only when she was on her deathbed that our family finally received closure and knew he was at peace. My grandmother passed on away on his birthday, and it was a sign to our family that he came to get her from the other side.

Chapter 3

My youngest aunt, Loretta, was more like a sister to me because a lot of my young life was spent living under the same roof as her. Yet, since she was my auntie she figured she could tell me what to do. She would threaten to put soap in my mouth when I talked back to her, but she never did because my grandma would always defend me and tell her to leave me alone.

Loretta mostly kept to herself and never had time for me unless I was getting on her nerves. Her space was off limits and her moods were sporadic, but when she was feeling up for company she would let me help her with one of her puzzles or take me for a ride in one of her boyfriends' fast cars.

I dreaded my aunt Loretta's going-out routine because it meant that my mom was going out too. When my aunt styled her bangs about three inches off her head and held them up with a ton of hairspray, I knew my mom and her were getting ready for a night out on the town. As they were on their way out of the house I would grab onto the sides of the door frame crying for my mom not to leave, while my grandma tried to hold me back by my feet. When my grandma would lose her grip on me, I would run after my auntie and try to attack her by pulling her long black hair. But it wouldn't stop them; they would still go out and forget all about my desperation while they danced it up at the Strange Range.

My mom soon ended up with a new boyfriend after moving back to Yellowknife. Ron had strong, chiselled facial features and a pale complexion. He sported a mullet and had a noticeable limp when he walked. Ron and my mom moved into a low-income row house unit not long after they met, and the plan was for me to move in once they were settled. It did not take long for me to realize that Ron was a mean and dangerous man. I would often opt to stay at my grandma's house because I did not like being around him. I remember one very vivid memory clearly because it was the day that I thought my mother had died. My grandma hadn't heard from my mother in a few days, so my grandma and I went to the house to check on her. My grandma must have known more than I did, because she brought a bucket and some cleaning supplies with her.

When we walked into the house, it looked like something out of a murder scene. There was blood everywhere, holes in the walls and broken glass from where a back window looked like it had been kicked in. Smeared blood led us up the stairs into the bathroom. The shower curtain was closed, and I held my breath and braced myself for what I imagined I would see. To my relief, the bathtub was empty. I thought for certain that I was going to see my mother's body beaten and left for dead. Instead, she was in the hospital suffering from a "fall down the stairs." This was the first of many instances of domestic violence that I would witness, breaking my childhood innocence.

I don't know why, but my mother stayed with Ron after that incident, and not long afterwards, we moved all the way across the country with him to a small town in northern Ontario, Ron's old stomping grounds. I could not understand why they were still together, since they seemed not to like each other, and I tried to ignore the constant tension in our house. I tried to pretend that I was living in a normal household and I would hold fast to the good times, as few and far between as they were. I sang and danced to the sound of the drum songs from the North in the living room of our split-level rental when we finally settled on a place to live, after weeks of having to live in Ron's mean mother's house where I wasn't allowed to make any noise and had to be on my best behaviour. It was exhausting not being able to be a kid. Ron's mother was excessively strict, and I wondered if maybe that was why Ron turned out to be the way he was.

I made friends easily at my new school even though I had super-short hair, oversized glasses and a poor sense of style, not to mention that I was trying to hide a huge secret at home. My glasses were chosen out of the small back section of the eye glass store, the Treaty section. The section that no one wanted because they were cheap, plastic, unfashionable glasses. I hated wearing glasses and, every time I got mad, I would throw my glasses down on the ground and stomp on them in a rebellious refusal of both the system that bound me to a certain class and the fact that I had bad eyes. But my anger was of no use to me, because my glasses would be replaced weeks later by another cheap, oversized frame at no cost.

My life in Ontario was somewhat normal, despite the domestic disputes that were going on at home. My friends and I would play marbles and jacks at recess and make fun of our mean homeroom teacher, who was adamant on making sure our handwriting was perfect.

After school, I would run up and down the block with my friends until dark. My mom never seemed to worry about where I was. She knew I was either at a friend's house, at the corner store buying frozen yogurt or climbing trees and jumping from roof to roof in back alleys. My friends and I would pretend to have mini concerts on rooftops and sing at the top of our lungs to our imaginary audience. I made sure I was always playing outside and never invited friends over, because I never knew when a fight might break out in my house. I began to subconsciously associate love with fighting and vice versa.

I kissed my first kiss on the stoop in front of my house. I prepared for that moment by practising kissing my arm one night. My friend told me it was the only way that I would learn how to do it properly. I felt so foolish trying to kiss my own arm, but it helped me to eventually build up the confidence to kiss my steady boyfriend after school one day. I spontaneously leaned over and kissed him. It was just a kiss on the cheek though, because I hadn't worked up the nerve to kiss him full on the lips. He was all flustered and surprised and said, "I have to go home for dinner," then ran for it, leaving me to wonder if I did it all wrong.

So, I had my freedom — but that meant that I was left alone a lot. The bar that my mom and Ron frequented was too far away for me to walk to, and I didn't know the way so I couldn't go and try to get her to come home. It wasn't like Yellowknife where I was used to standing outside of the Gold Range, waiting for my mom to come out and asking people to go in and tell her that her daughter was waiting outside. The regulars would usually just walk by and tease me, saying, "Isn't it past your bedtime? Go home you little Range rat."

On the rare occasions that my mom and Ron were home, Ron would play a game with me that he called "chicken" while my mom made supper. It was a risky knife game where he would get me to put my hand out on the cutting board and spread my fingers apart. He would quickly stab between each of my fingers, going around and around in circles with his sharp pocket knife. He had good precision but there were a few near misses. Ron never laid a hand on me unless I got in the way of him hitting my mom, which I often did. I would run and jump on him from behind to try to get him off her, but he would just shove me out of the way like he was swatting a fly.

One day that all changed when I was defending myself from Ron's unfair house rules while sitting on the edge of my bed. "Shut up!" I yelled at him, and without a word, he punched me clean in the jaw. I ran to my mother for help, but I couldn't talk because my mouth was stuck open. She was busy cooking dinner in the kitchen and didn't understand why I was crying and screaming because she didn't see what happened and he acted like he was innocent. My jaw loosened up after a little while and I could close my mouth again, but even now my jaw makes a weird grinding and clicking sound every once and awhile. After that incident, I couldn't help imagining kicking and punching Ron at night when I closed my eyes. I walked on eggshells for the next few months, until it ended abruptly.

❧

It was the weekend and I was out on a sleepover at a friend's house down the street from where we lived, when the phone rang in the middle of the night. The police were at my house. Ron had kicked my mother out with no shoes in forty below and wouldn't let her back in. After some investigation, I ended up as a ward of the government, a foster child in temporary care. When my mom came to visit me, the visits were short. We sat in a small, monitored room with glass windows where people observed us on the other side, taking notes like we were animals in a zoo.

The foster parents that I was placed with had a handful of foster kids from different families. Looking back now, I think it's safe to assume from the amount of foster children they had that they were only in it for the money. My bedtime was outrageously early, and my life was structured right down to the minute. Being on a strict schedule was something that I wasn't used to. I stayed in my room most of the time, drawing, colouring and just thinking of getting out and being saved. I felt like I was in jail. My routine was mundane: wake up, eat breakfast, go to school, do homework, go to sleep. I missed running around the block with my friends. I felt confined. My freedom was gone.

Shortly after I was placed in foster care, I was told that the nurses were coming to the school check our heads for lice. I was worried that I had lice because my mom had been treating my head before I was taken into care and I wasn't sure if it had worked. So, when it was my turn in line to get my head checked, I had to think fast. I didn't want the entire school to know that I had lice; it was bad enough that I was having problems in my personal life and I didn't want my popularity to slide. School was the one thing that was still going good in my life and I would have been absolutely mortified if my friends found out I had lice. Without thinking of the consequences, I keeled over and clutched my stomach acting like I was in severe pain. The nurses sent me to the hospital, where I had to undergo an enema. The doctors told my foster parents that I had a problem with my digestive tract and that I needed to be put on a strict diet consisting of high fibre, which meant that I had to eat soggy fibre cereal every morning before school. Turns out I didn't have lice, so the moral of the story is: don't ever lie or you might have to undergo an enema for safe measure.

Time went on and I began to wonder if I was going to be a ward of the system forever — or until I reached adulthood, which to me meant forever. Since I was in a different province than my grandparents, they couldn't come to my rescue and remove me from care. So, I waited. I waited for my mom to leave Ron and to stop drinking so that I could be back in her care again.

Each hour felt equivalent to a day for me, and after what seemed like a decade, the day finally came when I could go home. When my mom and I walked into our old house it was cold, half-empty and full of bad memories, but thankfully, Ron was nowhere to be found. My mom wrote Ron a goodbye note and left it next to a pile of overdue bills. She did one last sweep of the house as she slowly gathered her things to leave and I remember thinking that I couldn't get out of there fast enough. I stayed close to her side, impatiently tugging on her clothing trying to get her to hurry up. I was worried that at any moment Ron would barge through the door. Thankfully there was no sign of him, and my mom and I boarded the first train headed North without looking back.

I was so excited to be free again and on a train with a real conductor who would yell at me for running up and down the aisles, "For the last time, sit in your seat young lady!" It's a wonder we didn't get kicked off the train. We travelled for three days, until we reached the big city of Edmonton. In the city, we sat in the train station while my mom schemed our next move. Looking back now, I don't think she had thought through how we were going to make it all the way up North, but I trusted her completely as I followed her to the bus station. We boarded a dusty, dark bus with maroon-coloured seats and tinted windows, on route to Yellowknife where the trains don't run.

My mom ran into her childhood friend on one of our bus stops at a gas station outside of a tiny northern town that was swarming with blackflies and herds of buffalo. She was tired of being on the cramped bus and decided to ride the rest of the way home with him instead.

There wasn't much room in his old Suburban, so I had

to sit in the back on top of a large foamy. He had the back windows rolled all the way down as we sped down the old dirt highway that went on for what seemed like forever. When we finally arrived in Yellowknife, my hair was full of dust and sticking straight up. I couldn't even run a comb through it.

We were dropped off outside of my grandma's apartment building. My mom rang and rang the buzzer but there was no answer, so she told me to run to the local diner downtown to find my grandparents. I was embarrassed to be seen with my hair a mess, but I found my way to the diner where my grandma and papa recognized me before I saw them. They laughed at the wild child that I was and drove me home.

Chapter 4

*A*FTER WE ARRIVED IN YELLOWKNIFE, my grandmother became my primary caregiver and raised me in her small, one-bedroom apartment downtown. I slept on the floor over a thick, makeshift mattress made from blankets piled on top of one another to make it feel more like a real bed. I had red and yellow plastic milk crates stacked up against the wall to use as dressers for my clothes. We had one channel and no remote control for our small black-and-white television decorated with tinfoil antennas.

My grandma would stay up late working on the finishing touches on one of her delicious cherry pies or shuffling back and forth between playing solitaire and sewing while humming to herself and tapping her fingers on the table rhythmically. I always wanted to play cards with her, but she told me that I was too young to play cards at night. To her, playing cards and laughing at night were forbidden to children. She said that if a child plays cards late at night, the joker would dance around them in their sleep.

One night, my persistence must have annoyed her enough to change her mind. She let me play cards with her, but I soon regretted it because that evening I was scared to death of falling asleep for fear of seeing the joker dancing around me. Whenever I heard a noise, I would jump up in fear while my grandma snored away peacefully.

My grandparents drank quite heavily in their younger days, but my grandma quit drinking soon after I moved in and my papa followed in her footsteps not long after. They knew that they needed to be healthy and sober in order to raise me, and just like that, they stopped overnight. My grandma told me that her eldest son had visited her in a dream and told her to put the bottle down so that she could look after me, and she took that as an important message. From then on, my grandmother did the best she could to raise me. I always had clothes on my back and food on the table.

My grandma tried not to have store-bought meat if she could help it. She always had fresh caribou meat on hand and fried it up with a generous amount of lard so that I could soak a piece of bread in the pan grease afterward, for a treat. She would cut caribou meat into tiny, bite-sized pieces and put it on the side of her plate for me, and I would grab a piece, run away to play or watch T.V. and come back for more when I was hungry. Bannock and jam was dessert, and if I was lucky, my grandma would give me some caribou bone marrow, which is a delicacy, and dry meat with butter and salt.

It was easier to eat traditional food because it did not cost money. Sewing was my grandma's main source of income, but it was hardly enough to get by. She was hired by a local outfitting company that sat her in the back of the store in a little room, where she would sew up a storm. She was a humble woman, modest about her work, which is why she could never bring herself to ask for a raise. She never got the credit and recognition that she deserved for her hard work and was taken advantage of. She was underpaid, and her designs were imitated like so many Indigenous artworks that have been appropriated.

Nonetheless, she loved what she did and she always made time to make me fancy homemade parkas and mitts to keep me warm and show me off. But the fact that I had adorned beautiful, homemade Dene clothing gave some of the kids at school a reason to pick on me, simply because I looked different than they did. I wore my beautiful warm parka and mitts with pride until I realized that I was being made fun of for it. I started asking my grandma to buy me mitts and boots like the other kids had. I couldn't ignore the snickering in the hallway as I walked by, and I started to feel like a target. Even the teachers made comments on my garments and looked at me like I walked out of a different time zone. I didn't want to stick out anymore; I just wanted to look like everyone else and fit in. I didn't think for one second about how this must have hurt my grandma. She put in so much time, energy and love into keeping me warm. But, she didn't disagree with me and asked my mom to bring me to the store to get some new outdoor gear. After that, I went to school looking like everyone else. If I could have only seen then that all the lovely pieces she sewed together for me were priceless, and that I was blessed to have something that money could never buy.

❧

ASIDE FROM BEING BULLIED FOR how I looked, my behaviours and personality were attacked and made fun of by my elementary school arch nemesis Lindsay. Lindsay and I were in the same class. The first time I met her, she pushed me against the wall outside of the school during recess and the uneven rock siding sliced one side of my face open just below my eye. Lindsay would continuously find some reason to make fun of me, and because I didn't stick up for myself, it only got worse. One day in math class, she sharpened her pencil as pointy as she could just so that she could stab me in the leg with it when no one was looking, and the lead from the pencil broke off in my leg. To this day, I still have a noticeable piece of lead in my leg. It's a great conversation piece in the summer when I'm wearing shorts.

Lindsay's reign of terror didn't stop even when my grandma was nearby. One beautiful, sunny day my grandma and I were walking home from the corner store. If you live in the North, where our summers are short, you will come to know that these days are few and far between, so I cherished the warmth of the sun on my face as I skipped down the street ahead of my grandma. It was a particularly hot, arid day. Summers in the North are like the desert, dusty and dry. My grandma bought me a pop to quench my thirst. As I took a sip of my pop, from the corner of my eye I saw a girl with yellow hair and a ponytail swinging behind her come running at me with all her might, and then she shoved me from behind. I went flying and ended up lying on the sidewalk of Main Street with a deep gash in the palm of my hand from the can of pop that I was holding, which skidded underneath me. My grandma yelled Dogrib obscenities at this little, seemingly innocent girl who was laughing and running away. Mind you, if my grandma wasn't as stout and hefty as she was she probably would have gone running after Lindsay, but instead she helped me up from the sidewalk and dusted me off.

This type of bullying went on for years until, finally, I stood up to her. I told my best friend's dad how afraid I was that, any day, she was going to beat me up after school, and he gave me one of the best pieces of advice I ever got. He said, "Let her throw the first swing. After that, it's self-defence." It never occurred to me that I could fight back and defend myself. Being given permission from an adult to protect myself was just what I needed to be brave.

As my best friend and I walked home from school the next day, I looked behind me and, sure enough, the entire class was following Lindsay, who was following me. I wanted to run away, but I held my head high and stopped in the back alley of the school. I took a deep breath and turned around to face my adversary, and we were soon surrounded in a classic fight circle by our peers. I went through what I had practised over and over in my head the night before, and I envisioned what I would do when Lindsay hit me. There's something about fear that drives a person out of their comfort zone and forces them to do things that they wouldn't otherwise dream of doing. Up until then, I hadn't ever gotten into a real fight.

Words were said, her face was in my face, and after she threw the first punch I didn't hesitate for one second. I grabbed Lindsay by her blonde ponytail, the hairstyle that she wore every day of her life, and swung her around until her feet practically lifted off the ground. She landed in a heap next to a garbage can crying, embarrassed mostly, I'm sure. "It's not fair, you didn't fight fair!" she yelled. I didn't care if she thought I had fought dirty. She hadn't been fighting fair for years. I was nothing less than exhilarated and pumped full of adrenaline. A new life had just been breathed into me and, somehow in that three-second girlfight, I became a different person — or maybe it was already in me and Lindsay had just awakened it. Whatever the case, I was grinning ear to ear as I left Lindsay leaning against the garbage can wondering what just happened. I didn't know I had that kind of strength in me; only a few minutes before the fight I was trembling and possibly about to pee in my pants.

Looking back, if there is one thing I learned that day, it's that everyone is in our lives for a reason. Lindsay was in my life to shake me up and make me tough. I can now come to terms with the years of cruelty, shame and bullying that I under-went and all the days that I dreaded going to school afraid of Lindsay's wrath, because those hard times prepared me for even harder days ahead.

☙

MOST SUMMERS I WOULD BE shipped off to northern Alberta to spend time with my aunt Clara and my first cousin Rae. Rae and I looked a lot alike, but she was smaller than I was and had beautiful, long, thick, black hair from her dad's Inuit side. Rae was a year older. She was always one step ahead of me and made fun of me a lot, but since she was my family she had to love me and take it easy on me.

One summer, my aunt Clara and her husband planned a road trip up to Alaska. They had bought a little camper trailer and got it ready for our big trip up the Alaskan highway. Our road trip was a memorable one. Rae and I didn't appreciate the scenery as much as her parents, but we had fun panning for gold and roasting marshmallows whenever we stopped to set up camp for the night along the way.

On one of our stops, we set up camp in a place

Catherine and Rae
dressed up on Halloween
(photo credit Norine Lafferty)

just outside of Whitehorse. "Catherine, can you come with me to the outhouse?" Rae asked. "I'm scared to go alone." I was happy to be of assistance and proud that she needed my companionship. I followed her along the wooden-planked pathway leading up to the outhouse. "Can you look inside first?" she asked. "Sure," I replied without a second thought.

I opened the door and looked inside to make sure it was safe. That's when I realized that, right above me, in the corner of the outhouse was an angry hornet nest. I turned to run and saw that Rae was already on the other end of the path, looking back and laughing at me in her mischievous way.

I was too slow for the hornets; they caught up to me and stung me in the back of the head with what felt like a round of gunfire. I had to sleep on my face with a swollen head that night, and the dead hornets had to be picked out of my tangled hair one by one.

The wildlife really loved me that summer, because on that same trip, I found myself face to face with a moose. I was skipping along on the trail in front of everyone else, not paying attention to where I was going, when not more than one foot in front of me stood a moose calf. The calf looked like he came straight out of a cartoon. He literally had a piece of straw hanging out of the side of his mouth and was chewing it sloppily while a swarm of black flies formed a perfect halo around his head. When my aunt saw that I was too close to the calf, she made hand signals for me to back away slowly. The cow was in the bushes about fifteen yards away and was rearing up to charge at me. The bushes were swaying, and she was making a noise that only a mama moose can make when her babies are in danger. I got away just in time, or I would have been trampled.

When we reached the city of Anchorage, Alaska, we headed straight for the mall. As we were checking out of the department stores, we felt a rumble beneath our feet. At first, we thought it was an earthquake, but when we walked outside we were in a thick cloud of eerie black ash. The city that was bustling only a few minutes before was silenced. We were smack dab in the middle of a volcano eruption. We went back to our campsite, and everything was coated in three inches of soot. It was an unnerving scene that looked like something out of a horror movie. We quickly packed up our campsite, scooped some of the ashes off the picnic table and kept them as a souvenir. Then we started our long journey home, with Rae and I singing along with the radio to the latest country hits the entire way.

Years later, I was hosting a barbecue on Canada Day when my mom got an unexpected call from my aunt Clara. When she got off the phone she said, "Rae is gone," and the tears came rushing out. Rae was one of the most honest people you could ever meet. She was to the point, blunt and unapologetic. I'll forever cherish her competitive nature and her cheeky wit. She made the rules to all of our childhood games, and I followed. She will always have a place in my heart.

Chapter 5

At around age twelve I decided I wanted to live with my mom, to my grandma's disapproval. My mom was living in an apartment on the other side of town by herself and always had people coming and going. Living with her meant that I had free reign to do whatever I wanted. My mom was never any good at discipline. She leaned toward the side of neglect, though not on purpose. She was blinded by her own issues, and her honest effort at sobriety was short lived every time she tried. Since I had the place to myself most of the time, I had friends over often and we would hang out in my room and listen to music. That was the point when my life took a turn for the worse, and the quiet, reserved girl was replaced with a gothic, experimental troublemaker. I started smoking cigarettes and pot. At school, I could be found in the smoke pit trying to be like the kids that I thought were cool. Only I wasn't cool, and neither were they; I was a wannabe. As in any school there are the classic generalizations, different groups classified by their attached stereotypes. I didn't know which category I fit into.

In my first year of middle school, before my bad girl image took over, I hung out with the "smart kids" but I never fully felt that I belonged. I knew I was as smart as them, but I was on a different level than they were. It was undeniable when I would go over to their house to visit, because they always had the seemingly perfect family, expensive clothes, signed up for all the costly extra-curricular activities and had all the luxuries that I lacked. They grew up not knowing what it was like to go without. This made me self-conscious and, even though they didn't judge me, the invisible divide was always there. So, I slowly separated myself from them and started hanging out with the kids that I felt more comfortable with, because I could relate to them. We were on the same level. The kids who were smoking and acting up in school seemed to have the same issues as I did, and soon enough I could be found in the smoker's pit in the bushes around the corner from the school.

My homeroom teacher expressed her concerns to me after school one day and said, "Catherine, what is going on? You are one of my best students. I'm worried about your slipping grades." But, by that point, I was uninterested in doing well in school because I had nobody to hold me accountable to anything, and I was beginning to become more interested in fitting in than passing tests.

I became friends with Mandy, a girl across the hall from my apartment. Mandy convinced me to try smoking her mom's pot stash, which she kept hidden underneath her mattress. Soon enough, I was smoking pot daily. We hung out in Mandy's room listening to grunge rock and playing Ouija board. We even went as far as trying to summon our favourite rock stars from the dead, but the board started spelling out the word "devil" instead. We got so freaked that we threw the Ouija board, but not before the fire alarm was mysteriously set off next to the door of my apartment unit and I was blamed for it.

Fire is a powerful, unworldly element. My mother's house burnt down when she was a kid. My mom is certain that it's because she took something from a graveyard and brought bad luck home with her. She told me never to take anything from a graveyard because of what happened to her. She and some friends wandered around the Back Bay near the shore of the Great Slave Lake on the grounds of the old cemetery, where the graves are now slowly rising to the surface because they were buried on a hill next to a small creek that eventually started to run through the graves, rotting the wood and exposing the caskets and bones, disturbing the peaceful corpses. She and her friends came across a small, wooden box and, when they opened it up, they found a miniature silver fork, knife and spoon. They divvied out the utensils and my mom ended up with the spoon. Not long after, my mom's house burnt down and both of her friends experienced unfortunate tragedies in their families. When my mom's house burnt down, she told me that the only thing left standing was a large picture of the last supper that was hanging on the wall next to the rosaries, which were barely singed.

THE DAYS AND MONTHS WENT on, and the sweet, nerdy, pale, Dene girl with big, ill-fitted glasses, baggy clothes and bad home perm started acting out. Soon enough, I was labelled as a bully. I eventually got kicked out of middle school and was court-ordered to transfer to a different school. It was all because I thought a girl at the school was starting rumours about me. Well, that didn't sit well with me, so I decided to have a little chat with her in the hallway after school was out. I ended up pushing the girl into a fire extinguisher that was mounted to the wall outside of the music room. The music teacher must have heard the commotion because he ran out of his classroom to see what was going on and tried to stop the fight, but I punched him and got away.

I knew I was in trouble and that it was only a matter of

time until someone was going to come looking for me. I ran straight to my apartment and hid. Not long after, the police were at my door. I opened the door and slipped past them, booking it down four flights of stairs without even touching the steps. I slid down the railings until they caught me in the lobby on the first floor and held me to the ground while kneeing me in the back to keep me from squirming.

I was hauled into the back of a cop car with my hands behind my back, and it seemed that the entire apartment building stood outside on their balconies watching the drama unfold. From there, I was transferred to the police station jail cells, where I would stay confined for a couple of days in a small cell with one toilet in the middle of it and no privacy whatsoever. It isn't a death sentence, but when you are in it, it feels like a lifetime. I didn't leave the cell for fresh air, food, showers or visitors.

When it finally came time for my court appearance, I got the infamous one phone call. I called my mom. "Mom, can you bring me some clean clothes? I'm at the police station, in case you are wondering where I've been." Out of all the clothes my mom could have brought me that day, she thought a sweater with a large picture of Mickey Mouse on the front would be appropriate attire for a court hearing.

To make matters worse, the same day I was sitting in the small court cell waiting to be called in to appear before the judge was the same day that my class was on some sort of field trip to the courthouse. One by one, my peers opened the small window of my cell door and got a perfect view of the mess that was me. I felt like a caged animal on display. I couldn't hide from it, either. I suppose I could have crouched down under the bench and curled into a ball hoping no one would recognize me, but that would have only made things worse. Some kids I would wave at and some I would glare at depending on who it was. Some would stare at me a lot longer than they should have. I was a Mickey Mouse character all right. I moved back in with my grandma after that fiasco. But the careless, wild child within me didn't stop there. I was just getting started.

❧

I STARTED TROUBLE WHEN I WAS BORED. I would run up and down the hallways and get my grandma eviction notice after eviction notice. My grandma got numerous complaints and eventually got kicked out when the new landlords took over the apartment. Before the new landlords came along, we were somewhat safeguarded because I was best friends with the previous landlord's granddaughter, Bree. Bree and I became best friends when I first started living with my grandma. I think we got along so well because we both came from similar circumstances — our mothers were not in the picture very much.

I was severely bored one day and I was in one of my typical emotional, dark, raven-like moods. I invited myself over to Bree's place, dressed in black and wearing my shades even though the short, bright winter daylight streamed in through her living room window. I was in a phase where I teetered on the edge of the other side. I didn't think my life mattered. I didn't think about the future and who I could be. I only thought about the now. I couldn't see past the problems in my life. I had no hope for brighter days ahead. That day, I came up with the dreadful idea of raiding Bree's grandmother's medicine cabinet.

Bree's grandma had a variety of prescription pills, and I took a few from each bottle. I held the colourful assortment of pills in my hand — mostly diuretic, I'm sure — and without thinking of the consequences, I threw my head back and let the pills slide down my throat. The next thing I remember, my mom was shaking me to wake me up and bring me home. "Catherine, wake up! Get up! What's wrong with you?" She slapped me hard in the face and managed to get me on my feet, steering me toward the door before I walked head first into a wall. Lights out.

I woke up three days later. I slept through Christmas. As it was, Christmas was a hard time for us in our house. My Christmases consisted of Salvation Army Santas delivering presents and food bank donations in black, shiny garbage bags, so it wasn't exactly a magical time in my house. For the most part I was content to have presents and all the trimmings of a Christmas dinner, but what I loved most about Christmas was going to the midnight mass with my grandma and being allowed to open one gift before bedtime, usually a new pair of pajamas or socks. I never complained about not having a lot of presents because my experience of Christmas was never about abundance. And that Christmas in particular, it was anything but. My family was at a loss with me. I was out of control.

That was the same year I started seeing a boy named Mathew. We met at the uptown arcade. Yellowknife had two arcades back in my younger days. One arcade was located uptown where most of the rich kids hung out, and the old arcade was where most of the poor kids hung out. It was no coincidence that most kids who hung out at the downtown arcade were Indigenous.

Mandy dragged me to the new arcade one weekend, against my will, and I met Matthew. Matthew was also a troubled kid and he was sent to Yellowknife to live with his aunt and uncle. That year, we both lost our virginity while we listened to loud heavy metal music in his bedroom.

When his caregivers found out that Matthew and I were starting to get serious, they decided that Yellowknife was no better than his own home and he was forced to move back home with his parents. It was so hard to say goodbye to Matthew. I tried to sneak him into my house and hide him in my closet so that he wouldn't have to leave, but my grandma found him hidden under the covers and kicked him out in the cold. Half-frozen, he stubbornly serenaded me under my bedroom window, calling out my name, and looking pitiful.

After he left town, we would talk on the phone for hours and hours. Since my grandma's phone was strapped for long-distance calls, I had to use my friends' phone to call him. I didn't consider or care that the long-distance charges would rack up as much as they did. When my friend's dad — who kept his immaculate, shiny, vintage motorcycle smack dab in the middle of his living room with a small, wire fence around it — found out that I racked up his phone bill, he was furious, to say the least. It's safe to say I never went back to his house. I did, however, make up my mind that I was going to run away to be with Matthew, and when I make up my mind there's no turning back.

I scrounged and saved enough money for a one-way ticket to see Matthew. By the time I arrived at his house, I had ten bucks to my name. I had hopped a bus that took four days to get to the far end of Vancouver Island with nothing but a false sense of hope that, when I got to Matthew, everything would be great and we would live happily ever after. Boy, was I wrong. When I finally made it to Matthew's house, I realized just how far away from home I was. A homesick feeling sunk in the moment I met Mathew's mother. She was not fond of me, and it was glaringly obvious. She looked me up and down in a judging manner — my belly top, purple hair, thick black eyeliner and army boots. The way she looked at me made me feel ashamed of my sense of style.

By the end of my short visit to Matthew's parents' house,

both Matthew and I were thrown out on the streets of his hometown with no money and just a small inkling of hope that our young love would be enough to solve all our problems. We lasted a day on the streets. Darkness was setting in on us and we had nowhere to sleep and nothing to eat. I called my grandma with my last quarter to ask her to buy me a ticket home. "Grandma, I need your help, I'm on the street," I said, but she couldn't help me. After all, she had little money to spare, only enough to get by from day to day. She scolded me with her angry worry: "What's wrong with you? Why did you go that far in the first place? Get home!" I had no choice but to phone social services and ask for help. I reluctantly said farewell to Mathew and headed back to my cold little corner of the Earth.

Chapter 6

WHEN I RETURNED TO THE North after my runaway adventure, I was right back to my unruly self. I was a regular at the arcade, playing my favourite tunes in the jukebox and beating the boys at pool. I hung out at the arcade until closing time almost every day.

No one in my family knew how to handle me. I was completely out of control. That's when I realized that there might be one more person that could save me from myself: my dad. It took me three days to find his phone number in the large Toronto phone book. I lost a lot of quarters in the pay phone trying to find him, but I ended up finally pinpointing him through his sister. When I got up the nerve to call him, the conversation was awkward. "Hi, dad? This is … your daughter." Silence. Loud silence. He didn't know what to say at first. He told me he had a family. Two stepsons. He had met his new partner only a few months after my mother had left. He paid my way to come and visit him and his family, a few weeks later.

I arrived in the Toronto airport with my bright orange hair, black lipliner, short shorts and ripped tights. I did not resemble the sweet little red-headed girl with the pretty pearl hoop earrings that he knew years ago. I wonder what he must have thought seeing this presumably tough little girl with no cares in the world. He couldn't have known that the hostility I displayed while I was visiting that summer was a replacement for my longing for a stable life, like the life he had been living that whole time. The life that I could have had. He was a good father. I was happy that he had a family but, at the same time, jealous that he had started over without me. Undoubtedly, my visit was short lived because I felt like I didn't belong in his life anymore. The words we used to say to each other, "I love you more than the whole wide world," were so distant, they might as well have been way out in space. I wish I could have reached out and grabbed those memories, but, if I did, I would only end up drifting alone for eternity, trying to search for something that wasn't there anymore. So, instead, I gave up and ran in the opposite direction.

❧

YELLOWKNIFE FELT LIKE AN INCREASING burden on me and I would have done anything to try to get out, but running away and hitchhiking doesn't get you very far when there is only one road out of town. My friends and I would slowly make our way to the mall from the arcade to check things out and then turn around and walk back to the arcade. Continuously walking in a loop all day long was the only form of entertainment for teenagers with a lot of time on their hands and no money.

Sure, I could have been in school trying to bring up my grades, but that was no fun; plus I was so far behind in my studies from skipping school for so long that I would have to put in twice the effort. Combined with the fact that all my friends were out having a good time, school was low on my list of things to do.

I began a short-lived attempt at stealing, which consisted of trying to lift clothes and makeup, but I made for a horrible thief. My friend was sporting some nice clothes and told me that she got her clothes from stealing. I wanted in, so she brought me to the mall and we stuffed our backpacks with clothes while pretending to try stuff on in the change rooms. The store clerk was suspicious and called security. The mall security chased us all the way down the street until we hid in the back alley behind a crummy motel, huffing and puffing and trying to empty our bags before we got caught. Ever since then, I always feel like I'm being followed when I'm in an expensive store. I can feel the clerk's eyes on me and I instantly start to feel like I've done something wrong. It's the same feeling I get when the police are behind me and I am afraid I'm going to get pulled over, even though I've done nothing wrong.

Looking back, I only stole because I didn't know the consequences, and once again, I had to learn the hard way. I have always liked having nice clothes, though, so on my fourteenth birthday my friend enticed me to spend my birthday money in Edmonton on a shopping spree. She told me that her mom lived in the city, so we would have a place to stay when we got there. All I needed to do was buy a plane ticket and save a bit of money for shopping. I only had enough to buy a one-way ticket, but I wasn't concerned with how I was going to get back. I should have known it was too good to be true. The minute we touched down in the city, she unexpectedly brought me to a party out in the suburbs. I was turned around and lost. The people at the party were loud and rowdy. I felt so out of place, because deep down I was a shy, lost little girl who was far from home and didn't know anyone.

I sat in a corner of the room, keeping to myself while everyone partied around me. In the middle of the night a guy with a bandana around his head came waltzing in with a rifle stowed in his baggy jeans, bragging and laughing about how he had just scared an old man underneath a car and stolen his money at gunpoint. My anxiety hit hard, and I thought that if I didn't act like I fit in he would try to intimidate me too by pointing the gun in my direction.

The next day I told my friend that I wanted to go home. I couldn't dare stay at that house another night, so I told her I'd rather stay in a shelter. I checked into a youth shelter in the inner city, and my anxiety spiked through the roof. I felt so small, lost and alone. I was more afraid than I had ever been before. I managed to borrow enough money for a cheap bus ticket home. It was April and the ice on the rivers and lakes was rapidly melting, but the bus driver pushed on over the ice road, and as we crossed the mighty Mackenzie, he assured us passengers that it was safe enough to drive on. The bus was half submerged in the melted water that pooled on the surface of the ice, but we made it across safely, to everyone's surprise. Not long afterward, the bus starting slowly filling with smoke. The water had gotten into the battery, causing it to leak. Everyone on the bus had to hurry off and huddle in the cold on the side of the road waiting for someone to come and help. When darkness fell, I hitched a ride home down the old dirt road that I had gotten to know so well, and I swore to myself that I would never run away again for as long as I lived.

⤳

I TRIED TO BE GOOD FROM then on and get my act together, but the white devil came knocking and, when I didn't answer, he broke in. The first time I tried cocaine, I didn't feel any different. I was at a small get together and it was casually in front of me on the coffee table. The lines were cut and ready to go, inviting me to try it. My friends were taking turns kneeling over and snorting it with rolled up fifty-dollar bills. Everyone around me seemed to be enjoying themselves; they started acting like they were weightless and invincible, dancing around the room with their hands in the air like they were floating. To be the only one in the room not doing it would be questionable, so I joined in, and soon enough, I was no different from everyone else, dancing around the living room in a trance and reaching for the ceiling.

I got in with the wrong crowd of people and started getting offers from older men for sex. That part of my life is a blur, a hazy nightmare. I think I chose to block those days from my memory, because that wasn't who I was. I was a lost little girl trying to numb my existence.

I don't know how it happened or when, but I became entangled in a prostitution ring that was happening in the middle of town in a well-known bar, in broad daylight. I had to testify on the stand, still considered a child in the eyes of the court. I had to explain in front of complete strangers what I had experienced in detail, the sexual predators that I had encountered. My family was not there, and I am grateful for that. However, I had no support and walked out of the courtroom feeling even more violated. This is a part of my life that I considered not including in this book, but I feel that it needs to be shared because there are many young Indigenous girls that are coerced into prostitution on the streets every day, and it goes completely unnoticed much of the time, even in a small town.

Leading up to that point, I happened to have no self-worth left and my behaviour was a cry for help. I was craving attention, but I only attracted the wrong kind and sank into a deeper mess than I was already in. My self-love was gone. It had disappeared somewhere between the unceremonious reuniting with my father and the realization that my mother was probably never going to be the mother that I needed in my life because she had her own struggles to deal with. Looking back, I don't blame her. I know she had a difficult life and was trying to numb her own pain. She never meant to hurt me, but she didn't see that her neglect had a direct effect on me. I needed her to be stronger for herself and for me.

My grandparents were too old to run around town looking for me. I was so out of control that I wouldn't have listened anyway, but they never stopped trying, and most importantly, they never stopped caring. My grandma was always there to welcome me home even if she didn't understand the extent of the lifestyle I was living. I know my grandma stayed up all night worrying about me, walking the floors and praying that I was safe.

My grandma's prayers must have been answered because, for some reason, I was spared from going further down the road of drug addiction and self-destruction. Cocaine was never something that I developed a strong addiction to. I mostly did it because it was an escape route and it was normalized by the people that I chose to hang around. I'm quite positive that I overdosed on it once after a night of partying, though. When I got home in the early morning hours, I dragged myself into the shower on all fours, throwing up white foam after throwing my clothes in the garbage in the hopes that it would signify my desire of leaving that lifestyle behind me. I found myself in some slim situations in those days, and I am thankful that I am alive — a little jaded, but still breathing.

I never did go as far as doing needles. I did come close once but changed my mind at the last minute. That was before I watched someone shoot up in front of me. I watched as he ripped the corner off a little white bag with his teeth and then cooked up the powder. He grabbed whatever he could find off the floor and wiped his needle prodded arm, trying to find a spot where his skin wasn't already broken. He stuck the needle in, wiped the remaining blood off with an old dirty sock, then threw his head back and grunted. It must have been an immense feeling for it to have such control over a grown man, but after what I saw I had no desire to find out for myself.

My grandma told me that she once got a knock at the door of her apartment late at night, and when she looked through the peep hole she seen a man dressed in a black suit. She had a bad feeling, so she opened the door just enough to talk to him through the chain and asked, "What do you want?" The man had a briefcase in his hand and was claiming to sell something. "Can I come in and show you?" he asked. She told him that she wasn't interested in what he was selling and tried shutting the door, but he insisted. She looked at his expensive suit and wondered where he had come from. Then she looked at his nails and noticed that they were long, pointy and black. She quickly slammed and locked the door, but he was relentless. He kept on knocking louder and louder until she yelled at him, "Go away!" and the knocking finally stopped.

❧

I DON'T REMEMBER HOW WE met; we were just two people that happened to be in the same place at the same time. Brad became my everything, and I gave him everything that I had to offer. Soon after we met, we were instantly in love and inseparable. From the moment we first met, we spent seven whole days together in a tent in his backyard, busy falling in love.

Brad had beautiful blue eyes, for which I am an instant sucker. He was a real troublemaker but also a homebody at the same time. He never went out to have a good time or socialize, because whenever he went out it turned into a fight or a full-out bar brawl, so he usually tended to just stay home, out of trouble.

When we were together, we were unaware of the world around us. We used to hike up to the cliffs a few miles from the local beach. One night, we had the crazy idea to jump in the lake in our birthday suits just for fun, not thinking that anyone would ever catch us. To our surprise, a family found us swimming naked in the early evening and threw our clothes into the water at us. We had to tread water to get into our wet clothes while trying to keep our dignity.

I was crazy about Brad, so crazy that I tattooed his initials on my hand in black Indian ink, right on the soft spot between my thumb and pointer finger. I ended up getting it covered over with a butterfly tattoo a few years later. The tattoo artist told me that he was used to seeing bad tattoos and did a pretty good job of covering it up for me, even though it was taboo to ink up a person's hands in those days. My only other tattoo is of a rose on my right arm. My friend Bree and I were bored one night — boredom seemed to be the motive behind all my bad decisions with Bree — and we came up with the wise idea to tattoo each other. I asked Bree to freehand a tattoo with a large heart, angel wings and a halo on my upper arm. It was far less than even what an amateur could do, and I was stuck with the distasteful tattoo until a few years later. When a friend and I met a guy that said he did tattoos out of his house, we went with the intention of covering up my horrendous homemade tattoo. While we sat around in his dingy basement, we had a few drinks and he went to work putting some roses and vines over my angel heart. When my tattoo was finished, my arm was bruised and sore and I was ready to go home, but my friend wanted to stay and drink because her and the tattoo guy seemed to be hitting it off. So, I just went home and left her there, not thinking anything of it. The next morning, she was crying at my door. She had been raped.

I was so mad at myself for leaving her there alone with him, telling myself over again that I should have never left her. I know now that it is entirely his fault, but victims often take part of the blame and I know my friend felt like it was somehow her fault, too. I have since gotten the tattoo covered up, but I will always feel for my friend and the hurt and the shame that she went through when I look at the roses and the thorns wrapped around my arm.

That's not the first or the last time that someone I know was raped and the attackers got away with it. One of my cousins was drugged in a bar in the mid-eighties. She was beaten, raped, shaved bald and left for dead, face down in an empty grave outside of town. She survived, but she will be traumatized for the rest of her life. My grandma always said, "Don't ever leave your drink alone!" and, when I found out what happened to my cousin, it made sense that my grandma worried so much. It could happen to anyone. Even though I heeded her advice, it happened to me, too, by someone that I trusted. After a baseball tournament one summer, I was invited over to a friend of a friend's place to have a few drinks. I was offered a beer, took a sip and the next thing I knew I could feel someone's hands down my pants and the burn of the early morning sunlight on my face, shining in on me from the living room window. I tried to get up and grab my things to go, but I couldn't move. I felt paralyzed. I couldn't open my eyes, but I was somehow able to get away and run out of the apartment and fall asleep outside on the curb while waiting for a cab.

❧

ACID WAS THE MAIN DRUG on the streets when I was a teenager. In those days, between hanging out on the streets and sitting at the top of the steps of the old abandoned building across from the arcade, there was nothing much else to do but to get into trouble and experiment.

The first time I took acid I was with Brad and some other

friends. We all thought it would be a great idea to canoe to a small island in the middle of a lake and have a fire. By the time we got to the island, the sun was setting and the island was swarming with thousands of mosquitoes. The mosquitoes were so bad we could literally hear them sizzling in the fire every time we threw a log in.

Acid heightened every one of my senses to the point that I felt like I had expert hearing, sight, taste and touch, and I didn't know how to deal with it all at once. We didn't stay on the island for long, but it was long enough for me to want to get off. At the very least, I was not having a good time. We ended up going back to Brad's house where we watched movies until the drug wore off.

The next time I did acid, I hesitated to take it at all because of the way it made me feel the first time. But there's something to be said about peer pressure. My friends were pushing me to do it, so I gave in. I ripped the little cartoon square in half, put one half of it on my tongue to dissolve and threw the other half away. I think that since I was doubtful to take it at all, the drug began to act against me — that, or the hit I took was bad. Either way, I was stuck in a living nightmare for the next few hours.

The acid hit me hard and fast. I looked at myself in the mirror in the arcade bathroom and my face looked deformed and blurry. When I leaned in closer to take a better look at myself, my face starting moulding into someone else's, someone I couldn't recognize. I ran out of the bathroom trying to tell myself I was okay, but that was only the beginning. The drug hadn't even fully kicked in yet.

My friends wanted to go to the park. To get there, we had to walk past a long propane tank behind a gas station in the middle of town, and I could have sworn I heard an echoing voice coming from the tank, but I couldn't make out the words.

The snapdragon flowers that we walked past started bending themselves toward me, whispering something that I couldn't understand. I tried to tell myself that it wasn't real. I turned to my friends to see if they were seeing the same thing I was seeing, but they were laughing and having a great time. When we got to the park my friends all started running around and playing tag; I, on the other hand, was so disoriented that I could barely keep my balance. The ground beneath me was moving like waves, and I felt like I was under water.

I wasn't too far of a walking distance from Brad's house, so I started slowly walking the little path behind the park that led to his house, trying not to lose my balance on the imaginary waves. I didn't even say goodbye to my friends; they were too busy having fun without me to notice that I was ditching. When I got to Brad's house, he was not in the mood for my usual games. He was growing tired of my wild behaviour, but I was desperate for his comfort and support. I needed to feel safe so that I could get my mind straight and out of the awful daze that I voluntarily signed myself up for, but he told me to go home.

I called my grandma and papa to come and pick me up. When I told my grandma that I was on acid she didn't understand what I was talking about and I repeated myself into the phone, yelling, "Acid, ACID! I'm on acid!" My grandma still didn't comprehend what acid was, but she and my papa finally agreed to pick me up and told me to meet them at the corner store down the street from Brad's house.

To this day, I don't know how I rendered the ability to walk to the corner store by myself in the dark. When I arrived at the set of lights to cross the street I couldn't tell if the lights were red or green, so I just started walking into the middle of Main Street with car horns honking at me and people yelling. I made it across and jumped into the back seat of my papa's town car, which sat idling on the corner. There was a song about angels playing on the radio and all I could think was, boy, do I ever need one of those angels watching over me right about now.

My grandparents had no idea what was wrong, but neither of them asked me any questions because I must have looked completely incomprehensive. My papa drove like a maniac to get me to the hospital as fast as humanly possible. He always drove like a maniac, but this was more so than usual. They had no idea I was on drugs. All they knew was that I wasn't acting right and needed help.

When I arrived at the hospital, a large, scary-looking nurse with a huge gap in her teeth hooked me up to a heart monitor, gave me something that I'm guessing was valium and said, "Get some rest, you're going to be all right." I finally fell asleep, then went home the next morning, relieved that it was all over and I was back to my normal self.

Chapter 7

WHEN I WAS FIFTEEN, I FOUND out I was pregnant. No one in my family had talked to me about safe sex and contraception, so I didn't consider how easy it was to get pregnant and Brad didn't seem to be worried about it either.

When I first took the test and it turned out positive, I put the entire situation in the back of my mind and tried to forget about it. I knew not to drink, though, and my friends started wondering why I was staying home on the weekends. Most other nights I would have been hanging out on the rocks on the outskirts of town, drinking overproof straight out of the bottle with no chase.

For the first three months of my pregnancy, I walked around town pretending like everything was normal. I had a bit of morning sickness, but that was nothing; I was used to being hungover and it was slightly the same feeling. The reality didn't set in until the day came when I couldn't do up my jeans anymore.

Meanwhile, Brad and I started drifting apart. I found out that he had been cheating on me. I was heartbroken, but I still had to take care of myself and the baby that was rapidly making its presence known.

During my first clinic visit, the doctor asked, "Have you thought about what you are going to do?" I didn't have a plan for what I was going to do once the baby was born and

I hadn't thought about it until the doctor brought it up. I was only thinking about getting through my pregnancy, not thinking far enough ahead to prepare for taking care of a real baby.

At that point in my life, I couldn't even take care of myself let alone a baby. And Brad was proving, more and more, that he wasn't ready to be a dad. My living situation wasn't ideal. I was living with my grandma in a housing duplex behind the local bowling alley. It was hard enough for her to afford rent and groceries, let alone support another child.

The doctor guided me through my options. Basically, I could keep the baby and become a single teenage mother, have an abortion or give the child up for adoption. My first reaction was to keep the baby, but my bleak outlook for a brighter future for both the child and myself made me strongly reconsider. I knew that, whatever was to happen, I wanted my child to have the best chance possible from the start. The last option made the most sense to me. I told the doctor that I would consider adoption. My doctor told me that requests for private adoptions were sent through the clinic and that, if I was interested, I could read up on the some of the families who wanted to adopt.

I left the clinic that day trying to avoid it all, but I had such a heavy weight on my shoulders. My decision would change my life and the life of my unborn baby. I just wanted to wake up and realize that it was just a dream, but my growing belly was a constant reminder that I needed to decide soon.

I was about five months along when I finally made up my mind. I felt that my decision would be best for everyone involved. I went to the doctor and asked, "So, what is this whole private adoption thing about?" I wanted to read up on the families who were looking to adopt. The doctor gave me a profile of two families, both about fifty pages long. The documents looked like a proposal that you would write for a business contract, but instead it was a proposal for a baby.

The first family I read about already had close to ten adopted children. They lived on a farm in a remote southern town. They seemed like nice people, but I couldn't imagine having the child being thrown into the mix right from the get go and baling hay every day at the crack of dawn. The second family was a middle-aged couple that lived in a small northern town, even further north than Yellowknife. The husband owned a successful company and the wife was a head nurse at the community health clinic. They had hoped for a child for years but were unfortunately not able to have a baby on their own.

I brought the paper home with me and I must have read it a hundred times. I pondered the idea without telling any of my friends or family. I finally got up the nerve to call the couple a few days later, and it was the bravest conversation that I have ever had. I didn't know what to say at first. How do you come out and say, "Hello, you don't know me, but I am considering you as a candidate for the job of mother and father to my baby"? It's not a typical, everyday conversation.

They turned out be overjoyed and, in no time, they were on a flight to Yellowknife to meet me. We had an expensive lobster dinner together and they offered to pay the bill — my pregnancy cravings were not cheap. Over dinner they asked me about my lifestyle. Understandably, they wanted to know if I was eating healthy, if I smoked, if I was drinking during my pregnancy. I was honest and confessed, "I'm really trying to live a healthier lifestyle. It's been easy for me to stop drinking, but I still have the occasional cigarette."

I liked these people. They seemed down to earth. They were the type of parents that I would have wanted. I didn't tell them at first, but I had already made up my mind. I was going to give my baby to these kind people, in hopes that the baby would be raised in a loving, stable home, something that I didn't think that I could provide. When I told my family and Brad's family about my decision, they were saddened but mostly supportive — and, either way, my mind was already made up.

During the next few months, my belly grew. I didn't watch what I was eating, and I was a balloon. I ended up almost doubling my weight. By the end of my pregnancy, I had gained ninety pounds. No one told me that you can't eat whatever you want when you are "eating for two" and that you are only supposed to gain twenty to thirty pounds. My flawless skin became adorned with stretch marks. I now have them everywhere, even behind my knees, but they are a part of my story and I've come to accept them.

I stayed with Brad through the first trimester of my pregnancy and he tried to be there for me when he could, but he was doing his own thing while I was at home living a quiet lifestyle that consisted of painting miniature collectible ceramic ornaments, reading countless comics and eating everything in sight to keep myself occupied.

When my due date rolled around, there was no sign of the baby coming any time soon. After about two weeks of being overdue, my doctor decided it would be best to induce me. The nurses broke my water with a long, scary-looking tool that looked like a knitting needle, but it didn't jumpstart my contractions. The baby needed to come out; she was so overdue that she was starting to use her bowels. Once my water broke there was still no progress, which meant no baby. She did not want to come out. The nurses set me up to an intravenous that gave me false contractions, and it was the worst pain I've ever experienced in my life.

I was hooked up to what I called the "contraction machine

from hell" for what felt like never-ending agony, while my cervix made little progress. I inhaled two tanks of laughing gas in a matter of a few hours — which does not make you laugh, despite the name. I was in and out of the shower, and the adoptive mom massaged my back with a tennis ball while I kicked and screamed in pain. I begged for the doctors to give me a Cesarean. Finally, after two days of excruciating pain, the doctors agreed it would be best for me to undergo an emergency Cesarean section. Later, I found out that I probably would have died in childbirth if I hadn't gotten the Cesarean because the baby's head was stuck in the birth canal.

When she was finally born, she came out sleeping. She didn't cry until they spanked her to wake her up; she was drowsy from all the drugs that I was given. She was a turkey, weighing almost a full ten pounds. When it was time for her to be handed over to her to her adoptive parents, she was whisked into the arms of her new mother while I looked away and the doctors went to work to put me back together.

The day after she was born, I was finally able to move around. It was early in the morning, before visiting time, when I decided to have a good look at this little wonder that I helped create. I slowly walked out of my room and down the long hallway to the nursery, where I stared at her through the window until the nurse waved me in. She must not have been notified that this was an adoption case and told me I could bring her to my room. I wheeled her to my room in her little glass basinet, unwrapped her like a present and held her face to mine, breathing in her sweet baby breath. I smoothed her full head of soft brown hair and gave her a gentle kiss on the forehead, because I knew it would be the only time I would ever get to hold her. It was my hello and my goodbye all at once, in a single moment that would last a lifetime. It was the hardest goodbye that I've ever had to say. I whispered, "I love you" into her tiny little ear, shaped just like mine, and welcomed her into the world.

The most difficult choice I have ever had to make was to wheel her back down the empty hospital corridor and back into the nursery to let her go, into the hands of someone else to raise. This gift, this mirror image of myself, was not mine to keep. She was going to a family that I trusted would love her as much as I would, and I loved her more than anything I had ever loved before. I had no expectation to love her, to have such a strong sense of protection over her, but I felt an instinctive maternal love. That morning, I felt the grief of what it is like to lose a loved one, but at that time in my life I knew in my heart that this was what I had to do even though I was at war with myself. It took all the strength within me to turn against my own nature and believe that this was what was best — maybe it was not what was best for me, but I felt that it was best for her and that was all that mattered. It was the most selfless thing I have ever done and will ever do.

As I was wheeling her back to the nursery, her new mother walked through the doors to the ward and saw me with her. She stared at me for a few seconds, and I could see the confusion and hurt on her face as she turned back around and hurried out the hospital doors and through the long corridor.

A few hours later, her lawyer came into my hospital room and asked if I had changed my mind. I sat staring out the window. I could hardly hear anything that she was saying — my world was silenced — but I knew what she came there for. I'm sure the lawyer was used to this type of thing happening all the time, and she must have prepared her clients for the possibility of me changing my mind. After she was done her spiel, I reassured her that I had not changed my mind, nodding slightly to hide my sadness when she asked, "Are you sure?"

When it was time for the baby to leave the hospital, I said

my goodbyes to her new parents. My family came, and they had a chance to hold her. I'm sure that they were also feeling sadness; it was like losing a family member. A grieving was taking place without death, only a longing for things to be different. I didn't hold her again, even though the opportunity was there.

When she left the hospital to go to her new home, to her new beginning, I was left with an empty void. My family asked me if I was okay before they left my side. I pretended I was fine, but I didn't move for a long time. I just stared at the little grey television that was hanging from the wall above my bed in the hospital room, where they kept me for a few more days. I could only wonder if this empty feeling was going to last for the rest of my life. If it was, I didn't think I could make it through the days.

I prayed that the missing piece of my heart would heal one day. I gave myself full permission to accept the decision I had made and to not regret it, but the depression found a way to creep in. I felt that it was easier to not talk about her unless I initiated the conversation. After she left, I forgot how to smile, I forgot how to laugh, for a long time. With time, I knew that my empty heart would mend, I just didn't know when. I constantly reminded myself that I did the right thing. Even though I wasn't looking after my child, I was now a mother.

❧

AFTER HAVING THE BABY, I SUFFERED from anxiety. I wasn't the same anymore. I felt like I didn't know who I was. I distanced myself from my friends and family and I didn't want to go out in public if I could help it. I kept away from social situations and large crowds. I felt like something was wrong with me. I was afraid and standoffish. When things got really bad, I would panic and think that I was dying. I didn't know what my triggers were; I didn't even know what a trigger was. Out of the blue, I would start feeling like I couldn't breathe, or like I was as small as an ant in the corner of the room. It was similar to how I felt when I was in the shelter in the city after running away; that same strong feeling swept over me and I felt like I couldn't concentrate on anything.

I felt the need to flee whenever I was in an uncomfortable situation but, after a while, I felt like I was just running from myself. I knew I was having panic and anxiety attacks, but I didn't know how to cope with them. All I knew was that the feeling would slowly pass. Now that I'm older, I've learned how to manage my anxiety and talk myself out of my fears. I have learned to acknowledge the fear. I have come to accept that I don't know what is going to happen next. I allow myself to enter my fears and tell myself that what I am feeling is not as bad as I think it is, and my irrational thoughts begin to have less and less power over me.

The fast transition from being a teenager to an adult had a tremendous effect on me, and the anxiety I developed was a sign that I wasn't on the right path. It was a sign that something in my life needed to change. I couldn't keep going the way I was going. Many people with anxiety try to mask their feelings by drinking, but that only makes it worse. When I was younger, I didn't know any better and that was exactly what I did.

The next few years, I struggled to find myself and slid back into my old habits. I was still an out-of-control teenager growing up in a small, isolated northern town. One weekend, a friend of mine was getting beat up outside of the arcade and I jumped in to try to protect her because she was small and outnumbered. One of the girls in the group jumped on my back, punching me from behind while I wriggled and threw my arms around, attempting to throw her off me. I finally backed her into a wall until she loosened her grip on me, giving me enough time to grab my friend by the hand and run for it. We booted it from the arcade, past the mall, past the Gold Range, all the way to my grandma's house behind the bowling alley.

My friend and I were out of breath by the time we got to my grandma's house. We ran inside and locked the door behind us. The pack of girls were hot on our trail and banged on the windows to get us to come out. My grandma — bless her heart — kicked me and my friend out of the house and said, "Go see what they want." She didn't want anyone breaking her windows. She was literally throwing me to the wolves. I slowly walked outside of the house to where the girls were there waiting for me in a classic gang formation. I walked into the circle, and the leader of the pack came up close to my face and spared me when she whispered, "You have five seconds to get back inside your house before you die!" I hailed her pity on me and, after they left, my grandma let us back in the house. She had been watching the drama unfold from the window, ready to call the police. She taught me a hard lesson in bravery that day.

Before that night, I was always getting into fights. I know what it feels like to be boot-kicked in the face and thrown down the stairs by simply underestimating a person's strength. I had my fair share of scraps in my teen years, but the one I will never forget is when I was sticking up for a friend outside of the Gold Range who was about to get beat up by a big, tough Dene girl known for beating up the boys. She punched my friend in the face for no reason, and I told her to back off and leave him alone. So, she turned her attention to me and started chasing me around vehicles while I tried to kick her and run away at the same time. She grabbed hold of one of my legs and took me down, sitting on me in the middle of the street, grabbing handfuls of my hair and trying to smash my head into the ground. I had to put my hand behind my head so she wouldn't crack my skull open. No one was strong enough to pull her off me, until a friend of mine saw what was happening and broke it up before the police came.

Where I come from, the girls are tough and know how to scrap. Maybe it's because we learn, from an early age, that we have to protect ourselves — because if we don't, who will?

Chapter 8

*Y*EARS LATER, AT A RANDOM HOUSE PARTY, I was being picked on by a girl that was disagreeing with everything I said until a guy named Jeremy piped up out of nowhere and started defending me by making fun of her. I thanked him, and he asked me for my number, but I was seeing someone at the time, so I didn't let him have it. A few weeks later, he showed up at my doorstep. My papa answered the door and came to my room saying, "Some big-eyed boy is here to see you." When I went to the door, I was surprised to see that it was Jeremy. "I had to ask around town who you were," he said. "Want to come to a party?" I was already in my pajamas so I turned down the offer, but I was so flattered that he went out of his way to find out who I was. So, I got a pen, wrote my number on his hand and told him to call me. He never did.

The next time I seen him, I asked, "Why didn't you call me?" He said, "I would have, but your number smudged off my hand." After that, he showed up at my place after he took home the gold medal at a weekend hockey tournament. He was a good hockey player and I couldn't help but be impressed that he wanted me to share in the glory, so I ended up sneaking him into my room and letting him stay the night.

I had a part-time job at the local newspaper around that time, and I was given absolute freedom to write about whatever I wanted. I wrote about things that I was interested in and, when I needed people to interview for a story, I approached my friends and family. I admit I was somewhat of a unadventurous reporter, but the way I saw it, at least I had a job that I didn't mind because I got to do something that I loved: write. I also got to play around in the dark room and develop my own photos, which was another outlet for me to express my creativity. The randomness of my articles included anything from interviewing my stepdad on his car-washing business to interviewing my grandma on her sewing. No life or death reporting or chasing down leads on the latest crime; I kept it close to home.

The reporting gig provided me with the money that I needed to save up for a car. I figured it was about time that I bought myself a car with my savings from work, since my papa never drove me anywhere; in fact, he used to make me walk through blizzards and whiteouts to get to school each morning when I was younger.

My papa was a cranky old fellow. He loved me, but he was always irritable with me and didn't know how to show his affection. The closest he got to showing he cared was when he would get angry at me if I did something wrong, voicing his disappointment by yelling at me. He must have turned out that way because of his life growing up. He never spoke about his family, but my mom told me that he had to walk for miles in his torn-up shoes to his little school house on the outskirts of his hometown.

When my papa did drive me anywhere in his town car, he was very particular about how I got in and out of the car. We were not allowed to slam the door; that was a big thing with him. And he would smoke, boy would he smoke. He smoked me right out. My papa was a chain smoker, so much so that when his ashtray got full, he would ash his cigarette in the bottom of his rolled-up jeans. He had a special ashtray in his car, the kind with the soft, checkered, beanbag bottom, and he would light one cigarette up after the other while I sat in the back seat on child lock, unable to roll down the window myself. When I said, "Papa, can you please roll down the window?" he would only roll the window down a tiny smidgen, just enough for me to reach the crack in the window so that I could purse my lips out as far as they could go and suck in fresh air for my survival. Those were the days before anyone knew anything about second-hand smoke, but I'm sure he wouldn't have listened to "all that nonsense" anyway.

I already had my learner's licence so, as soon as I turned sixteen, I was the first person in line at the vehicle registry to get my licence. I failed my first test by no fault of my own. The examiner told me to pass a vehicle while I was driving in a school zone. I didn't think twice about the speed limit and zoomed ahead to pass the vehicle beside me in the other lane. He said, "Okay, the test is over. Drive back to headquarters," and I thought to myself, "Wow, that was quick; he must have known what a skilled driver I am," but then he went on to explain how I had failed. The second time I took the test, I was asked to parallel park. I failed at parallel parking, but when we got back to headquarters I poured on the tears, saying, "I promise that I will never ever parallel park as long as I live." I think the driver examiner felt sorry for me, because I managed to get my licence that day.

When I finally got my licence, I put the money I earned from working at the paper toward a 1982, wine-coloured Thunderbird for a steal of a deal. And, just like that, I had my freedom and it felt ten times better than zooming down hills on my bike or walking in circles around town from the arcade to the mall. I was the only person in my crowd of friends that had wheels. I loved my old, beat-up, rusty Thunderbird. My friends and I would drive around aimlessly for hours, blaring tunes out of the cassette tape player. But everything has a shelf life, and my car happened to have a very short one. It lasted a little over a month. One day, when I was turning left on a green light on Main Street, it suddenly died on me and some passers-by helped push it to the side of the road.

෴

IN THE NORTH, BAR AGE IS NINETEEN. So, when I hit that prime number, you can bet your boots I was a bar star. I had been waiting for years to be able to get into the bar. I was never able to sneak in when I was underage, because everyone knew my family. My best friend Kristen and I had the time of our lives in the bar. We were the dancing queens; we owned the dance floor. Kristen and I met around the same time I met Brad. I was jealous of her when I first met her because I thought that Brad liked her. I soon found out that she wasn't interested in him, so we hit it off.

As young adults, Kristen and I had a lot in common. We could be ourselves around each other. We would sing into our hairbrushes to bad eighties music in her bedroom, rollerblade to the beach in the summer, read up on our horoscopes and try to meet each other in our dreams. We were both tired of living at home and thought that we were ready to live on our own. We rented a two-bedroom apartment together but realized quickly how different it was to live on our own and how each of us liked to have our own space. Even though we had been inseparable, being roommates didn't work for us. Kristen was reserved and quiet. She liked her space to be a place where she could have her down time, but during that time I was — let's face it — still a party animal and always wanted to have people over.

On Kristen's twentieth birthday we went out dancing, and

I found myself in the middle of a war between two guys fighting to take me out for dinner. One of those guys was Jeremy. Jeremy and I hadn't exactly set it in stone that we were seeing each other. We had only hung out a couple of times, and things weren't serious. A cute guy at the bar, who meant well, was trying to ask me out and take me for pizza. Jeremy must have overheard because he shoved the poor guy onto a pool table, holding him by his shirt collar and saying, "pizza smizza" with a serious look on his face. Jeremy invited himself back to my place after the bar, and we sat together and talked for hours. He wanted to stay but I told him that probably wasn't a good idea. Getting Jeremy to leave was difficult. I had to be mean and hold the door open for him to show him the way out. I didn't consider that it was super cold that night and that he may not have had anywhere to go. In the morning, I was worried about him and could only imagine him lying frozen in a snowbank, so I called around to make sure he was okay. His friends must have passed on the message that I was worried about him, because he was soon back at my apartment like a lost puppy and there was no getting rid of him after that.

Jeremy was the funniest guy I had ever met. He could make anyone laugh. He was always the life of the party wherever we went — scratch that, he *was* the party. Jeremy started hanging out at the apartment daily, but Kristen wasn't too fond of having him around because all we did was drink. Kristen and I inevitably ended up going our separate ways. We remained best friends but realized we were both living completely different lives. I ended up moving a few doors down the hall into a one-bedroom with Jeremy.

Things were great at first; we managed to dress up our little apartment and play house. I even had a computer. We had our fun but still managed our responsibilities like mature grown-ups. Jeremy took care of me on my twentieth birthday when I got too drunk in the bar and broke the heel off my four-inch stilettos. He had to carry me out because I was a mess and couldn't walk. He carried me home, tucked me into bed and went back to the fun.

At that time, I was enrolled in nursing school at the local college, and Jeremy was working as a labourer. I didn't take my studies too seriously and dropped out of nursing school halfway through. My excuse was that I didn't like the thought of having to give needles or see blood, so nursing was out of the question for me. However, I do give the utmost respect to nurses. It has got to be one of the hardest jobs there is.

My carefree, precarious lifestyle carried on this way for a few months, until one day I woke up and had a strong hankering for hot dogs. I don't particularly like hot dogs, but I managed to gobble down a whole package of uncooked wieners for breakfast, to my grotesque satisfaction. I knew right then and there that I was pregnant. I took a home pregnancy test to confirm my suspicions and, sure enough, I was.

When Jeremy got home that day, I told him the news. He didn't seem to be too enthusiastic. "We're not ready to have a kid," he said. He thought we were both too young, but I didn't listen to him. Jeremy was in his early twenties, and I had just turned twenty. We had only known each other for a few months. I told Jeremy that, whatever happened between us, I wanted to keep the baby. I stopped partying right away and expected that Jeremy would be on board with me, but he didn't change his ways. We started arguing a lot. I told him to get out, even though I didn't mean it. He took my threats seriously. As he was packing his stuff to leave, I said, "With or without you, I'm having this baby!"

After he left, I couldn't afford to keep the apartment on my own, so I ended up moving back into my grandma's house until I could figure out what I was going to do. While Jeremy and all my so-called friends were out gallivanting, I was at home alone, taking up knitting. I knitted the baby a cute, yellow mini-pillow and blanket. I was so excited for this baby. I knew that I was ready to be a mother, and I already loved him. Him. I knew in my heart that he was a boy.

Jeremy would come and go throughout my pregnancy and, like a fool, I would easily let him back into my good graces. I ended up landing a job as a receptionist with the government and rented myself a bedroom in a nice penthouse suite in the mall, off a man who won the lottery. He had purchased real estate all over the world and travelled a lot, so he was never around. The suite was great. It had all the amenities I needed, but I was lonely. I didn't eat properly. My main craving was eating sugary cereal before bed.

During the end of my pregnancy, Jeremy was willing to try to be a father. I'm not sure if he was back with me because it was a place for him to hang his hat or if he honestly cared. Whichever the case, I welcomed the company. Jeremy and I would go out together to the local pub on the weekends with his friends. We would sit at the bar together and I would watch him drink way too much whisky while I sipped on coffee to keep up. I suspect that this might have something to do with why my child is so energetic and can't sit still, even to this day.

Jeremy didn't make much money, but he saved up enough to buy me a cute little garnet promise ring to express his love for me. I ended up having to sell the ring for grocery money not long after because we were low on cash, but it was the thought that counted. If he had known any better, he would have known that garnet is not my birthstone. But, it turned out to be a significant coincidence that foreshadowed part of my future with Jeremy.

Before the baby came, I wanted us to have our own place rather than a rented room. Having a place to call home was more important to me than ever, because I was in the nesting stage of my pregnancy and I wanted to have a room ready for the baby. Jeremy ended up getting hired on at the diamond mine on a two-and-two rotation, so we could afford a nice, two-bedroom apartment near the lake. At that time, Yellowknife was booming from the diamond industry. The downside was that the mine was located way out in the tundra, and it was a fly-in, fly-out camp. Sadly, many of the families that have partners working at these mines fall apart. Jeremy and I weren't an exception to the rule.

I was alone most of the time in the new apartment building, even when Jeremy was in town, and I swear that it was haunted. Rumour had it that someone had hung themselves in the stairwell back in the eighties, and it's been haunted since. I would stay at the apartment during the day but, as soon as evening hit, I would leave and stay at my grandmother's house because of the fearful feeling I had in my gut. One day, after baking a batch of cupcakes to bring to work with me, I was leaving my house and trying to lock the deadbolt from the outside of the door. I could have sworn that someone was on the other side of the door, holding the lock. The creepiest feeling came over me and I threw the cupcakes in the air and ran down the empty hallway to the nearest exit.

I asked my cousin to stay with me one night so that I wouldn't have to be alone. We woke up in the middle of the night to the sound of the front doorknob violently rattling, like someone was trying to get in. The doorknob rattled off and on for a few minutes while we sat in the living room, frozen in fear. I was too afraid to move, so my cousin got up the gumption to check it out. She grabbed a knife for protection and quickly swung the door open, but no one was on the other side of the door. There wouldn't have been enough time for someone to run down the long hallway without being seen, and we had no explanation for what could have caused the doorknob to rattle. We couldn't sleep for the rest of the night, and I gave my move-out notice the next day.

❧

RIVER WAS MY PRIDE AND JOY. He was the roundest, cutest, happiest baby I had ever seen. I was overjoyed to have this little companion in my life to love and nurture, and he kept me on my toes. My motherly instincts kicked in immediately; there was no place in my life to be anything less than the best mother I could be. I just wouldn't be able to live with myself if I didn't put him first, before anything else.

Jeremy, on the other hand, did not change. I tried to get him on board with me, but he would disappear for days on end just to come crawling back, apologizing. The situation was not ideal, but I was willing to work on the relationship for River's sake. I wanted River to have his father in his life.

One night, while River was sleeping in his crib, we had a few friends over. Everything was going great. My girlfriend and I were out on the porch visiting with each other, while her boyfriend and Jeremy were inside watching hockey. I had no idea that they were scheming to leave us and go out. Before I knew it, Jeremy came up to the balcony doors and locked them shut. "Come on, open the door," I said, laughing and thinking he was playing a joke on me. But Jeremy and his friend merrily ignored us and walked out of the apartment. I watched helplessly as they jumped into a cab. Jeremy didn't seem to care for one second that our baby boy was inside the house, sleeping in his crib, while I was stuck outside on the balcony of our apartment. I panicked. My friend tried to calm me down, but we both didn't know what to do. It was only a matter of time until River would wake up, crying, and I wouldn't be there for him. I tried to break the glass, but it was too thick and I had nothing to break it with. The only options were to either jump off the balcony, hoping to land on my feet and not break my neck, or climb across to the neighbour's balcony and pray that I wouldn't fall onto the concrete below.

I slowly reached for the balcony beside mine, careful not to look down, and made it to the other side. The neighbours heard me knocking and opened the balcony door. "I'm sorry, but I'm locked out of my house and stuck on the balcony!" I said in a panic, and they let me go through their apartment to get to mine. Thankfully Jeremy hadn't locked the front door. I ran to River so fast to check on him, to make sure he was still breathing, since I was an overly cautious mother in the first place. He was sound asleep and oblivious to what was going on.

I was so angry that Jeremy would do something like that, without even thinking of the consequences. It was so uncaring and selfish. I'll never understand how an urge, an impulse, can be more powerful than the safety of your own family. I often blamed myself for Jeremy's behaviour. Maybe I did something to make him do that. Maybe I needed to be nicer to him. Maybe he just needed a break. Excuses, excuses. The truth was, I didn't know Jeremy. This was not the person that I fell in love with. I fell in love with a charismatic, vibrant, funny, protective man, but this Jeremy was someone I didn't know. His behaviour was unpredictable. If I tried to talk to him, I would be left defeated and confused. I started to think about the possibility that he was starting arguments just so that he would have an excuse to walk out the door.

Something needed to give, so I decided it was going to be me. I needed to make a change. I wanted to go back to school, so I started researching the options I had. Since I didn't graduate from high school, the doors weren't exactly flying open for me to attend the top universities. I found a school for esthetics in Edmonton that piqued my interests, and the requirements to get in seemed lenient; no high school education was required. I decided to give it a try and submitted my application; after all, it couldn't hurt to try. After a few weeks of waiting, my application was approved to attend school in the fall. I was going to be a college student after all.

When River and I arrived in the big city, I realized quickly that I needed to be on my toes. Down south, everything is go, go, go. In the North, it's the opposite. Everyone takes their time; they arrive late, leave early, no one rushes. Living in the city is like a rat race, always running from one place to the next because it takes so long to get anywhere.

I didn't exactly have a plan set in place before we left Yellowknife, and I didn't know where we were going to live. I just thought that things would fall into place once we got there. It wasn't as easy as I thought it would be to find a decent, safe apartment near my school. Since the school was right downtown, the affordable rentals were taken and the rest were ridiculously expensive. I ended up taking a chance on an expensive bachelor suite in a posh building a few city blocks from my school. Our tiny apartment was lonesome, but at least we had each other and that was all that mattered to me.

I placed River into a nearby daycare, which was situated in a government building. He was the youngest baby in the daycare, only four months old. I would drop off River in the mornings and speed walk to school, trying not to be late. After school, timing was always an issue because the daycare would lock their doors at exactly five fifteen every day and I couldn't leave the school until five sharp, so I would end up locked out of the daycare on some days, knocking on the windows and waving down the janitor to let me in. The daycare staff would give me the same lecture about being late for pick up: "You know you can't always be late picking him up, Catherine; we close at five."

There were times when I got so mixed up with my days that I couldn't tell one day from the next, because I would be so rushed and sleep deprived. I even thought I forgot River at home once. I was still in a dream-like state from exhaustion and called the daycare from school to make sure he was there.

The program I took was learn-as-you-go. We practised our skills on paying customers and, because we were still learning, clients received a discount price. I learned to do the basic spa treatments: pedicures, waxing, relaxation massage, facials. The only problem was, I wasn't very good at any of them. I lacked confidence as an esthetician and, as a result, I made a lot of mistakes on those poor paying customers. I have one too many horror stories of my days at beauty school.

One day a tall, dark, handsome and very hairy man walked into the spa to get his back waxed. I tried to hide in the back room and pretend I was busy cleaning the waxing pots so that my instructors wouldn't choose me to do it, but they knew I didn't have experience doing a back wax yet and thought it would be a good idea to place me with the hairiest man possible to fine tune my inadequate waxing skills. I hesitantly entered the small spa room with him and said, "Okay, so, ummm, just take your shirt off and lie face down on the table," trying not to turn beet red in the face. When he lay down on the table, the room suddenly got hot. I began to sweat, and my heart was beating out of my chest. I tried to focus. "I'm a confident professional," I told myself, but I was so nervous that my hands were shaking.

I just wanted to get the job over with as soon as possible, so I scooped a big glob of wax from the jar on the table next to him with my wooden spatula and smeared it down one entire section of his back. Any esthetician knows that you are only supposed to start off with small sections, not an entire strip. I smoothed a long piece of paper over the wax and rubbed it in to get a good grip on the hair but, when it was time to pull it off, I hesitated. You are never supposed to hesitate when you are waxing, never. The man yelled out in pain, "What the hell?" and turned around quickly with a snarl. "I'm so sorry!" I said. "It won't happen again." But I couldn't be sure.

The next time I tried, I closed my eyes and prayed that it would work, while beads of sweat rolled down my forehead. I pulled the strip, but I still had the technique wrong and his skin pulled up again with the strip. "I'm so sorry!" I apologized repeatedly. By that time, the paper was stuck to the wax and the wax was stuck to his back. "Please be patient with me, I'm just learning," I said, but that didn't seem to help with the situation. He was fuming and confused as to why I didn't know how to do my job properly. After what seemed hours of gruelling labour on both or our parts, I was finally able to get the last bits of wax off his back. He didn't end up paying for his service, and I don't blame him.

This client distress went on and on at the school. One woman came in the day before her wedding to get her sideburns waxed and, to no surprise of my own, I left her walking out with large purple bruises on both sides of her cheeks from not pulling the wax off fast enough, even after I had warned her that I didn't know what I was doing and there were no guarantees that I would do a good job.

Another woman came in for an armpit wax, but her armpit hairs were too short, so I had to manually pluck every single one of them out with tweezers, instructor's orders. Not everything was my fault, though. One woman came in for a pedicure because she thought it might help her with the severe frostbite she had on her toes. She was a runner and was doing a marathon in the mountains when her toes got so badly frostbitten that they turned a bright green colour. Northerners know all too well that green is the colour they turn before they turn black, and black toes mean they are dead and need to be amputated.

Catherine and her Papa at her college graduation

During my final days at school I became very skilled at waxing, and it ended up being my favourite service, ironically. When I graduated from beauty school, my papa flew to the city to attend my graduation ceremony. My grandma didn't come — not because she didn't want to, she just wasn't one for the city. It was too big for her.

Even though my papa would never admit it to me personally, I knew that he was proud of me. The graduation ceremony was an important day for me as I finally got to wear a real cap and gown, something that I had missed out on from not graduating high school. My Papa bought me a nice silver dress, sliver shoes and a matching sparkly clutch. He dressed up in his black leather jacket, slicked-back hair and aviator shades. He looked like an older version of James Dean, and I was proud to have him as my date. It was such a great moment for him as well; after that he would always say, "You're going places kid, you're high class." He was one of the few people in my life who believed in me and knew how important it was to get an education. No one in my family had graduated from college, let alone high school, and he had placed his hope in me to set the bar high. He put me on somewhat of a pedestal after I graduated. I wanted to prove to my papa and to the rest of my family that I would make them proud, live up to their expectations and go after my dreams. I wasn't only doing this for myself anymore. I was doing it for them.

꙰

WHEN I RETURNED FROM SCHOOL, I returned to the old apartment that Jeremy and I had shared before River and I left. Jeremy and I had a deal that he could keep the apartment while we were gone and that we would remain in a long-distance relationship and see how things would unfold when River and I returned home.

My graduation present from Jeremy was a cushy, king-sized bed, and the first thing I did when I got home was dive into it. I felt like I was floating on a cloud. I had never had a brand-new bed before, let alone a king-sized, pillow-top mattress. The second I lay down in it, I was out like a light. I must have been so exhausted over those last eight months that I finally had a truly restful sleep. That peacefulness was short lived because I soon found out that, while I was in school, Jeremy hadn't changed his ways and we found ourselves right back where we started. Shortly after I moved home, he packed up and left.

Life was simpler and undisturbed with just me and River. I found work at a spa and was practising my trade. We developed a suitable routine, but it wasn't long after we were back in Yellowknife that I noticed something out of the ordinary on River's body while giving him a bath. I took him to the emergency room that night to get him checked out. The emergency room doctor said that he could have hurt himself somehow while running around. It made sense; after all, he was a pretty rambunctious kid. The doctor said, "The swelling should go down in a few days," so I took his advice and thought nothing of it.

A few weeks went by and the swelling was still there, causing River a lot of discomfort. I brought him to our family doctor, who immediately sent us in for an ultrasound. Both the doctors and a specialist confirmed that it was a tumour that needed to be removed right away. The next day we were on a flight down south to the children's hospital in Edmonton, so River could get an operation. When we arrived at the children's ward, the doctors ran tests on River. I felt helpless having to hold him down while the nurses poked and prodded him. He looked at me through his tears as if to ask me, "Why?" He was too young to understand what was happening to him. When he came out of the operating room, he was heavily sedated, but as soon as he saw me he jumped off the stretcher and into my arms, saying "Mommy" over and over. The tumour that was removed turned out to be cancerous, and they kept us in the hospital for more than a week to run more tests on River to see if the cancer had spread throughout his body.

It was heartbreaking being in the children's ward of the hospital. Most children admitted had some form of rare cancer. We shared a room with a girl River's age that had undergone brain surgery. Seeing a young child — who should be full of life and able to run around and play outside — confined to a hospital bed for days on end, sometimes months, and hooked up to an intravenous tube with toxic, neon-green juice running through their veins was unbearable, and seeing how sick the chemo made kids was an eye-opening experience. Chemotherapy is a double-edged sword. It kills the cancer cells, but it also kills the good cells at the same time. Most of the children in the ward were very lethargic; they had no hair left and black rings underneath their eyes.

I told the doctor that, if River needed chemo, I wanted to try to treat him first with traditional medicine at home, and if that didn't work then I would bring him back for the doctors to administer their Western medicine. But they would not allow it. They brought in a social worker who told me that they would have to take River from me if I did not provide him with the proper health care. I felt afraid and did as I was told, even though I felt threatened and alone.

Waiting to find out if the cancer had spread was the longest week of my life. I felt hopeless. River's health was now out of my control and the only thing I could do was pray. I was not one to pray but I prayed to the only God I knew that the surgery was successful and that the cancerous cells were removed so they didn't spread to other parts of his body. I prayed that he wouldn't have to undergo chemotherapy. I prayed so hard that I promised God I would do anything if He would just let my son be healthy. I tried to make a bargain with Him because I was so desperate. I have never prayed so much in my life.

A week later, the doctor said that the cancer hadn't spread and that River was going to be okay. There was a one percent chance that the cancer would come back throughout his lifetime. I was so relieved that I broke down crying. I had tried to keep it together the entire time we were in the hospital, trying to be strong while we waited for the results, and when we got the news that he was able to go home, I was overwhelmed with happiness and forever grateful that my prayers were answered.

❧

A FEW MONTHS AFTER RIVER was released from the hospital, I decided I needed a break — a stress-reliever — and made plans to go out on the town. I ran into Jeremy in the bar and I happily ignored him for most of the night, knowing that he was watching me have fun. I liked knowing that he was bothered by the fact that I was not showing any interest in him at all. And, like a replay of the "pizza smizza" episode, a random guy tried to hit on me and I could see Jeremy from the corner of my eye lurking around me like a shark circling its prey. Before I could scream, Jeremy had jumped on the guy from behind, throwing him off his chair and getting my full attention. Jeremy was thrown out of the bar, and I foolishly followed him to see if he was okay. When he saw that I had followed him, he punched an innocent parking metre and smashed up his hand. I felt sorry for him, so I let him back into our lives. I brought him home and bandaged up his hand and his ego.

Not long after, I ended up pregnant again but had a miscarriage. It had been days since I had started losing blood, and it got to the point where I couldn't ignore it anymore. I was feeling very woozy and took a shower hoping that it might help. I was so weak that I fainted trying to hold myself up. Jeremy must have heard me calling for help from the living room where he was watching T.V., but my voice was so faint that I felt like I was in a dream where I was trying to scream but no noise would come out.

He helped me out of the shower, wrapped one of my arms around his shoulder and carried me to the bedroom, where I flopped over onto the bed. He tried to pick me up and get me dressed to take me to the hospital, but I had no strength; my body was lifeless. My eyes were open, but I could only see black. Jeremy was standing two feet in front of me and all I could see was darkness. I reached out and felt around for him. He thought I was joking and said, "Stop playing games and get dressed," but I couldn't. My lips were blue, and my body was going into shock. Jeremy carried me to the car and drove me to the hospital, where the emergency room nurses immediately wheeled me into surgery.

When I opened my eyes in the hospital after the surgery, I saw an angel. The angel was in the form of a man with large wings and a golden gown. His entire aura was golden yellow. He was hovering above me with his wings spanned out. No sooner had I seen him than he was gone; he faded up into the hospital wall and disappeared somewhere into the heavens. It all took place in less than an instant. I thought I was dead, and the peaceful feeling that came over me was insurmountable. I was enclosed in a blanket of peace, love and comfort. In that minuscule second, I wasn't worried about anything. I had let go of every single fear I ever had. There is no way I would have ever wanted this for myself, to die so young and leave behind my son. To feel at peace with death was something foreign to me; I was not ready to go yet, but that second of divinity I experienced made me want to stay there forever. I now know that there is more than this life, and that realization is calming. It is the ultimate reassurance. Looking back on that day, I still wonder if maybe I had woken up too soon, before I was supposed to. Or, maybe, I was supposed to catch a glimpse and tell others so that they could have hope and believe. Whichever it was, I am grateful that I got the chance to see my guardian angel.

When the angel disappeared, I heard someone shuffling next to me and I managed to mumble, "Am I dead?" The nurse checking my vitals must have heard me, and she said, "No, you lost a lot of blood but you're going to be okay." That's when I realized that I wasn't dead; I was lying in the recovery room of the hospital. I was admitted for a week after the surgery and very close to needing a blood transfusion — I had lost more than half of my blood.

Chapter 9

I HAVE A WANDERING SOUL — this I know for sure, because I can't stay in one place for too long. I need constant change. I need to see new things. My desire for movement must have stemmed from my childhood. When you get too used to being in one place for too long, you start to fear leaving that environment, so you never take chances or step outside into the unknown, which is why I never like to get too comfortable.

I was getting bored working as an esthetician, and I never had the passion for it to begin with. Truth be told, the whole spa thing was starting to drain my energy. I wished that I could be pampered for once and afford to have my feet massaged and my nails done, but I was living on a fixed income and struggling to stay afloat.

After my near-death experience, I realized that life is too short to waste it, so I started considering a new career path. I applied to a few college programs down south that sparked my interest. I read an advertisement for an Indigenous social work course. It was a one-year certificate program that could lead into a two-year diploma. It was a program that I thought I would feel comfortable in because I would be learning about my culture and how to help my community. I applied and was easily accepted. That fall, I hauled all my belongings back to Edmonton, where River and I spent the next year of our lives. Although he was invited, Jeremy chose to stay behind.

As a young mother alone in the city with a young child I often felt afraid and vulnerable. River and I lived in an apartment building downtown and I always felt that I needed to be on guard. The high crime rate in the city was something that I wasn't used to. Our apartment building had minimal security and it made me uneasy that we could be easily broken into because we lived on the second floor, but I never thought that I would have to worry about my neighbours.

We had shared laundry facilities, and one day while doing laundry I patiently waited for someone to take their clothes out of the dryer. Hours had gone by and it was clear that the person must have forgotten about their laundry, so I took it upon myself to put their clothes on top of the dryer, put my wet clothes in and go about my day. When I went back to get my clothes out of the dryer there was an obscene note left behind for me. It worried me that someone could be so angry and I was afraid as I walked back down the hall to my apartment with my laundry basket. After reading the threatening note I was extra cautious and watched my back, but the note was just the beginning.

Shortly afterwards I noticed spit on the outside of my apartment door and would often have to clean spit off my car. The worst part was, I didn't know who it was that hated me so much or if it was just a random coincidence. Either way, I became suspicious of everyone on my floor and I wondered if it was because I was a woman or I was Indigenous or both.

My school was located in one of the shadier parts of the city. It was a small classroom squished between a bike shop and a pawn shop; if you drove by and blinked, you would miss it. There were only five of us in the class and, at the end of the year, only three of us graduated.

One evening, the school invited me and River to a Round Dance at one of the local colleges. River got so worked up when he heard the drums that he started dancing and taking all his clothes off, right down to his diaper. I didn't notice what he was doing until I looked down at him. The rhythm of the drums flowed right through him. He had the beat of the drum in his heart. His ancestral DNA was awakened. River has always been strongly connected to his culture. He knows how to pluck a duck and gut and scale a fish like a local expert, even though no one has ever taught him how.

River never did have a solid male role model in his life to look up to. He had my papa, for a time, and even though he didn't teach River bush skills, he would come and visit me and River in the city often. Whenever he told us he was on his way to visit, we would be so excited to pick him up at the airport. Growing up, my papa was not known for his generosity. On my birthdays, he would dish out five dollars and tell me to spend it wisely. He was stingy with his money, which is why he had so much of it saved. My papa had scrimped and saved the money he made from an illegal business, which he carried on for years right out of his little one-bedroom apartment. My papa was a bootlegger, and everyone knew where to go for off-sales come closing time. In Yellowknife, the liquor stores are closed early on weekdays and closed on statutory holidays. The only place you might be able to get a drink on a Sunday is at church, so my papa made a very good living selling off-sales.

I found out about his business when I was still a young girl living with my grandma in her small apartment, after I broke in through his living room window and snooped around in his apartment one day while he was out for coffee with my grandma. He never let me into his apartment, and I would have been as good as dead if I was caught, but I knew his daily routine and that he wouldn't be home for a while. My papa always walked around with big wads of cash wrapped in rubber bands in the back pocket of his jeans, and I was curious to

Catherine and her Papa sitting on the porch outside of her house in Ontario (photo credit Norine Lafferty)

know how much of it he had stowed away.

Along with finding rolled-up bills under his mattress, I also found dozens of bottles of whisky and vodka stashed away in his bedroom closet. Instead of taking the money, I grabbed three mickeys of cheap whiskey, called up my two best friends and told them to meet me up on the rocks behind our apartment building, just up the way from the old folk's home. We sat and drank until we couldn't stand anymore, stumbling around trying to help each other up. We polished off two of the three mickeys between the three of us — who, altogether, weighed less than a grown man — and passed out in the hot summer sun. When we finally gained back a bit of our balance, we helped carry each other home. To this day, I can't smell whiskey without gagging.

On one of his visits to the city, my papa noticed that my car didn't sound very good and said, "Let me to take it to the shop for you." When I met him after school at the dealership, he said, "Go pick out a car," and pointed to the lot. While I was at school, the mechanic told him that my car wasn't worth fixing, and I was better off trading it in. My little, beat-up car, which I had bought second-hand when River was born, had been just enough to get me from point A to point B, but it was not reliable, and it was falling apart on me.

As I walked around the lot looking at vehicles, I was expecting to hear him tell me he was joking. But he walked along with me and helped me pick one out. No one in my family could believe that my papa bought me a vehicle, but he did, and he bought it in rolled-up, hundred-dollar bills wrapped in an elastic band in the back pocket of his rolled-up jeans because he didn't trust banks to hold onto his money.

I hold dear to my heart the times when he came to visit me and River. We would often go out for Chinese food in the restaurant of the hotel that he stayed in while he was visiting. I can still hear him call River "the boy" in his husky voice as my papa tried to get his great-grandson to laugh by making funny noises at him. I think having River around helped my papa deal with the loss of his sons. I can't imagine how my papa and grandma must have felt having their boys leave this world so soon. Children are good for the soul and having River around was very healing for my papa. I think River filled his life with so much love that it made him forget about his sorrow. He lightened up around River and forgot what he was ever angry about.

❧

WHEN RIVER AND I WENT back home for Christmas break, we spent it at Jeremy's mom's house. She lived in a beautiful home a little ways out of town, and it was a nice getaway from the hustle of city life. One night, on Christmas Eve, I saw a bright, white light about fifty yards outside the window of the loft bedroom. It was about four in the morning and I was the only one awake. I stared at it for a few minutes, until it started slowly moving toward me. At first, I thought it was a helicopter, but it didn't make any noise. I became afraid and closed my eyes, hoping that it would go away. When I opened them again, it was slowly making its way back up into the atmosphere, fading out of sight. In the morning, I told everyone what I had seen. "You wouldn't believe what I saw last night!" I tried to describe it as best I could, but they thought I was just trying to get them excited about Santa and his reindeers, so I gave up trying to explain.

Jeremy was there that Christmas, and we reunited once again. That was also the Christmas we got stranded out at the cabin. Jeremy, his cousin, my girlfriend and I made plans to skidoo to the cabin and spend the night there. The cabin was across the big lake and over a few portages, about an hour and a half snowmobile ride. There was a break in the weather that night. Most of the week it had been in the minus forties and fifties, so we were lucky to have minus thirty with no wind chill. Jeremy was in charge of getting the skidoos ready, and I was in charge of the food. As overly cautious as I am when it comes to being out in the bush, I had packed cans of food and supplies to last us the entire winter, just in case we had any emergencies. Jeremy scoffed at me for bringing so much food, saying, "What are you bringing all that for? You would never know how to survive in the bush!"

When we got out on the big lake, one of the skidoo belts broke, but it was a quick fix. "Too easy," I thought to myself. We started up again and, on our second portage, our skidoo light slowly died out and the skidoo came to a gradual stop. Jeremy's cousin and my friend were behind us on the trail and we could see their skidoo light wane, too, seconds later. Jeremy had forgotten to put gas in the skidoos.

When I asked the obvious question, "Did you fill up the skidoos before we left?" Jeremy got mad and took the bag I had packed full of food and supplies and threw it around and around over his shoulder, like he was practising to throw a shot put, and chucked it into the bushes. Everything came flying out and scattered in the snow. I just stood there, staring at him and shaking my head.

We all met up in the middle of the small pond between portages and tried to figure out what to do. I was the only one who wanted to go back, and I was outnumbered because walking across the big lake would have been too cold. If we stayed in the trails, we would be sheltered from the wind — plus, their rationale was that the beer was already at the cabin. So, we hunkered down and started walking the long trek toward the cabin under the starry sky and the northern lights, stopping every once in a while for a break.

It took us four hours to walk to the cabin and, right before we turned the corner to the cabin, Jeremy's cousin dramatically fell to his knees, saying, "I can't go on any further!" We all laughed at him and told him the cabin was only a minute away. When we got to the cabin, we were pretty much stranded because we had no cellphone service. I tried to have fun and make the most of the night as we played board games, drank too much and warmed ourselves by the wood stove. The next day, Jeremy and his cousin left us girls at the cabin while they walked in minus fifty to go get help. They were rescued by a hunter who was checking the trails; otherwise, I don't think they would have made it back without freezing to death or, at the very least, losing some fingers and toes.

The way I see it looking back now, throughout an entire decade of my life, wherever I went, Jeremy was never far behind. He would be drawn to me like a magnet when I was doing well for myself. Inadvertently, he stole my positive energy so that he could use it to build himself up. He would completely drain me of my ability to live until I only had a drop of life left in me, and then he would disappear again only to resurface when my batteries were fully charged. This was our cycle. Our honeymoon phases never lasted long. The explosions always grew more intense than the last time. Things continually got worse for us the more we tried. We were both moving in completely opposite directions. I was starting to shine, while his light was slowly fading.

Like everyone else our age, I liked to have a drink or two, but I never binged. Waking up and drinking again after a night out was the last thing that I could think of doing, let alone actually stomach. Because many people in my family suffer from alcoholism, it is almost a sure thing that I am an alcoholic, too — but, for some reason, I can go weeks and months without having a drink or even craving a drink. The problem is that, when I have one drink, I usually can't stop until the night is over and I'm dying of a hangover the next day.

I know myself well enough to realize that I can't just have one or two drinks and call it a night like the "sophisticated" drinkers you see having one glass of wine at dinner. Once I have a drink, I feel like I can drink like I used to when I was a teenager. I tend to consume way too much and end up hugging the toilet seat in the morning, wishing I never drank in the first place and promising myself to never drink again. Because of this, I try to stay away from alcohol altogether; it has never been a friend to me or anyone close to me.

Like a never-ending rerun, Jeremy ended up moving back to the city with me and River after the Christmas break to try to reconcile. We both thought it would be a good idea for him to get out of the same old scene. We both thought that maybe we needed a geographical cure. We did good for a while. Jeremy found a full-time job after sucking up his pride and opting to work at a gas station down the road from our apartment until he could find a better paying job. I think it was a very humbling experience for him, and I did give him credit for trying. He went from making five times the amount of money he was making in Yellowknife at the diamond mines to pumping gas for rich folks, driving the fancy cars he could only dream of owning one day.

Jeremy was a good father to River, when he was around. River had cut his own hair one night while he was being baby-sat. I had to shave his entire head so that his hair could grow back evenly, and Jeremy shaved his head too so that they could have the same haircut.

Shortly after River's third birthday, I got pregnant with Brooke. River didn't know it yet, but his little life was about to change; he was going to be a big brother.

❧

FIVE MONTHS INTO MY PREGNANCY, Jeremy returned to Yellowknife for work. He had found a better-paying job back up at the mine farther north. I was left to pack up our apartment with River by my side and a growing belly. I didn't enrol in my second year at the college because I was due to have the baby in the middle of the school year. When River and I arrived in Yellowknife, I heard the rumours that I didn't want to hear. Jeremy had been fooling around on me, and it broke my heart. When the time came for Brooke to come into the world I did not allow Jeremy to come to the hospital to see her because I was so angry at him for what he had done.

Brooke was born in the coldest month of the year, and her arrival made me complete. Her birthstone was a garnet, which reminded me of the ring that Jeremy had bought me when we first started out on our journey together. It was a symbol of our time together and how she was so perfect and meant to be, no matter what life threw at us.

When River came to the hospital to meet little Brooke for

the first time, he didn't want to come into the room. He stood around the corner of the hospital room door while everyone came in to visit and meet the new baby. He would peek in every couple of minutes, with one eye on Brooke. But every time someone saw his little, round face, he would quickly hide. He wasn't sure what to think of her yet and had to scope the situation out first. When he finally did come into the room, he sat in the corner and quietly coloured a picture, looking up whenever someone made a fuss over the baby. The next day, he got a bit closer to have a look at this tiny mirror image of himself and handed Brooke the same picture that he was busy drawing the day before. That was his gesture of love, his offering. By the time Brooke and I were able to leave the hospital, River was holding his baby sister, dressing her and even helping to change her diapers.

Being a young, single mother with one wild little boy and a baby that cried all the time was very difficult. When Brooke cried, it was amplified. Her cry sent a ping right through me. This must be the karma that I was due from putting my mom through so much agony when I was a baby.

River was a handful to begin with, but he started acting out a lot after his sister was born. He would do very odd things to get my attention. He purposely peed in a small, toy teacup and said with his cute little baby voice, "Here mom, I made this especially for you." I thought it was a game of pretend and he had gotten some water from the tap, so I played along and took a sip only to realize that it was pee. It took all my patience not to get angry at him, but I wondered why he would do such a thing while smiling at me and looking so sweet. He had been fully potty-trained for years. The last straw was when he purposely peed on the beautiful, white, rabbit-fur moccasins that my grandma had made me and stained them yellow. That was the first time I yelled at River.

Times were tough, and since I wasn't working, I was barely making ends meet. I had been taking a few online university courses at the time, and I filled in for a receptionist on maternity leave, which provided me with some extra income but also made it difficult to juggle my responsibilities as a mother. I often did my course work at night in between Brooke's feeding times and relied on friends and family to help me with the kids so that I could write my exams.

Jeremy really wanted to see his daughter, so a few months after she was born, I gave in and let him visit. He pulled up to our house in a big semi-truck that he was driving for his new job, but he didn't think about how he was going to get out of the tight parking space that he drove into and it took him two hours to back out. Jeremy always knew how to make me laugh and forget why I was ever mad.

We all moved into a trailer together shorty after, and Jeremy and I shared the costs of paying market rent, helping to pay off our landlord's mortgage. Jeremy's mom owned a nice, big house in a historic part of town on the waterfront. Jeremy had grown up in the house and his mother had been renting it out. Jeremy asked his mom if we could move into the house — it only made sense — so she let us rent the house at a decent price.

The house was huge. I had never lived in a big house before and it took a lot of getting used to, especially keeping up with the housework. It had five bedrooms, a big basement, and a nice deck with beautiful views of the lake. I recognized the house as soon as I stepped inside; I had dreamt of the house before ever seeing it. Not as in it being my dream house — I had specifically had recurring dreams of the house.

As I've gotten older, I've noticed that my dreams often come true months, sometimes years, after I've dreamt them. I like to think that it's the universe telling me that I'm on the right track in life, sort of like a premonition or a déjà vu. In my dream of the house, I saw myself standing in the basement long before I moved into it. Each time I dreamt of the house I would go one step further into the basement, and I would eventually be alone in the dark with only a small bit of dusty light beaming through a window in the corner.

Despite this premonition, things were going well, for once. I worked from home and had a spa set up in the basement. Even though I knew it wasn't my calling, it was money that we needed. Business was good. I was starting to get some regulars lined up and, I didn't love what I did, but at least I was able to work from home while the kids were small, which I did love.

My papa ended up moving in with us. He had long quit his bootlegging business and was having a hard time making ends meet. He was done with being fined one too many times. He had his own room in the house, and he would constantly complain that it was too cold and have five portable heaters running all at once — a fire hazard waiting to happen. Right next to the heaters sat his spittoon can. Since he wasn't allowed to smoke in the house, he chewed tobacco instead.

Even though he lived with us, my papa would still go visit my grandma every day. She would cook him dinner and he would come home usually after midnight or whenever he started to get tired, sometimes two or three in the morning. In the mornings, he would pick my grandma up in his fancy town car and she would dot her bright, rouge lipstick on her cheeks. They would drive around town for hours, always ending up parking their car outside of the Gold Range. This was their routine, day and night, for as long as I can remember, and when my papa moved in with me, it didn't change much. He was never home, except to sleep. I would hear him coming in through the back door at night so as not to wake anyone.

He would forget that there was no smoking allowed in the house, and one day while I was upstairs, I could smell the faint smell of a cigarette. So, I quickly made my way down the steep stairs leading to the main floor to lecture him about smoking in the house again. "Papa, are you smoking in the house?" I was in a rush because I had to get set up for work. I had a coffee in my hand, and when I got less than half way down the stairs, my feet slipped out from under me. My coffee went flying as I hit every single stair on the way down.

When I reached the bottom, I thought I had broken my back. Jeremy and my papa stood over me, trying to help me up while I lay there wriggling and crying. I had fractured my tail bone. It put me out for a few weeks, so I needed Jeremy to help me with the kids. But he had made plans to go out of town on a hockey tournament that day and wouldn't have cancelled it for the world.

❧

THE SPA WAS STEADY BUT not terribly busy and, apart from being a mom, I needed a hobby. My kids were my entire world and I loved them more than anything, but I also needed time for myself. I made it a point to discover what it was that I liked to do, what made me truly happy, apart from my family. I wanted to find my passion.

Growing up, I took the time to write in a daily journal. I never did hang on to my journals. I usually ended up burning them or tearing them up as a symbol of healing myself from the past and moving onto the next chapter of my life. I would often write poetry or just rhyme random thoughts and write about the things I was going through at the time, but I never thought to turn my writing into art.

I didn't know the first thing about how to play an

instrument, but I knew how to put together the structure of a song. Songwriting came naturally once I got started. I think the sorrow in my songs came from the buildup of emotions that I had kept inside of me, and they flowed out of me. I was creating harmony instead of indulging in something destructive. The words soothed my soul. I had countless songs presenting themselves to me, just waiting to come alive.

I was determined to learn how to play guitar, to start creating my own sound. Jeremy bought me a guitar and I started to teach myself how to play at night, while the kids were sleeping. I wanted to go into music when I was younger, but it wasn't something that we could afford. My mom made the effort to put me into piano lessons once, but it was no more than a few lessons, not enough to learn the basics. On the guitar, I taught myself the three basic chords that I needed to string a song together. I wasn't the greatest singer in the world, but I knew that I had some good material for songwriting, so I put my words to a melody. I started branching out to other musicians around town and, before I knew it, I was welcomed into the local music scene.

I would go to open mic sessions around town where I would expose my soul to small audiences that were respectful and patient, knowing that I was just starting out. Some nights I would play better than other nights, but I didn't care. I played for free and it was a way for me to gain some control of my life, get out of the house and socialize with other artists. I applied for a grant to produce my own album, since I had written enough songs to do a full-length set. After a year in the studio, recording almost every night, we managed to put together a full-length recording. It was such an arduous process. At the end of the day, I wasn't happy enough with it to release it. To ask people to pay for my less-than-quality music didn't seem right, so I wrapped it up with nothing to show for it except some stage experience, which at least got me over my fear of speaking in front of crowds.

I gave up trying to be a musician, but I promised myself that, when my kids got older and my life slowed down a bit, I would pick up the guitar again because my love for creating music would never fade. It's just another avenue to tell a story in my own words. I'm sure I drove my papa crazy, learning how to play guitar every night above his bedroom. The kids would plug their ears whenever I belted out a tune, but I didn't care. It was something that was for me. It was a way of finding my own identity amid being a mother, a caregiver and a wife — or, playing the part of what I thought a wife was supposed to be.

Chapter 10

FOR THE FIRST TIME, JEREMY AND I had a consistent go of things without breaking up or fighting. We even started talking about marriage. After all, we had been together, off and on, for almost ten years. My grandparents weren't getting any younger, and I wanted them to see us get married. I started dropping hints to Jeremy.

I ignored every piece of advice that anyone ever gave me. Friends and family warned me not to get married to try to fix a relationship. Deep down, I knew they were right. I have such a strong intuition, but what good is that if you completely ignore it. I was good at ignoring red flags and obvious problems, because I didn't want to accept that I couldn't have a happy family with the father of my children. I was too proud to admit that I had grown up and left a broken home only to find myself back in the same situation. I wanted to have a normal family — or be some version of what I thought normal was supposed to be.

Jeremy got a discount on a small diamond ring from working at the mine. The ring he chose was very inexpensive, but it was all we could afford at the time. I didn't mind. It was discounted because it had a huge flaw in it that you could see with the naked eye. You didn't even need a microscope to see that there was a large black sliver smack dab in the middle of the diamond. It was a perfect reflection of our relationship.

When Jeremy proposed, it was a different kind of memorable. Jeremy was not a romantic person; even the word "romantic" made him want to throw up. He told me he was going to propose over dinner that night and I thought it would be sweet having the kids with us when he popped the big question. We were supposed to go out for a nice family dinner at a fancy restaurant, but we didn't make reservations in time. So, we opted for a fast food restaurant at the last minute. I anticipated him pulling the ring out at any moment, and I was bracing myself the entire dinner. But he never did ask.

When we walked into the house after dinner, Brooke had to go to the washroom. She was being potty-trained at the time and had just missed the potty and peed all over the bathroom floor. While I was in the washroom, cleaning up the mess and down on all fours, Jeremy thought to propose. I was coming out of the washroom with the potty in my hands, the kids were running around the house screaming and Jeremy was standing in front of me with the ring in his hand. It was all over in a matter of seconds and wasn't as big of a deal as I expected it be. There were no violins playing in the background, no happy tears, no opportunity to leave him hanging while he was down on his hands and knees, wondering if I would say yes. I don't think he even asked me at all; he just nonchalantly put the ring on my hand. As disappointed as I was, I still said yes, and life went on. I got the kids ready for bed and he called his cousin up on the phone, half-jokingly saying, "Hey buddy, well my life is now officially over," while channel-surfing the television with his feet up on the coffee table.

❧

JEREMY AND I INVITED EVERYONE we knew to our wedding. It was the wedding of the decade. Every single small-town character showed up and then some. We didn't have much money, so we had to be creative. I had my dress custom-made by a Columbian seamstress that couldn't speak much English, but she was affordable, and I heard that she had created gorgeous, one-of-a-kind pieces for a few other brides in town. She sized me a few months before the wedding, and I told her that I wanted the dress to hang a bit off my shoulders to cover my tattoo.

I thought we could cut costs for the wedding by serving traditional food instead of paying for catering, but Jeremy's mother insisted on paying for the food, so I didn't argue. Instead, we cut costs in other ways. I made the invitations myself and included a beautiful quote on the perseverance of love, as I thought our relationship to be the epitome of persistence, if anything.

We decided to get married outside of town at a little tourist area that was fully set up with teepees. It was all coming together. I had five bridesmaids and Jeremy had five groomsmen. My dad was even coming into town for the wedding, which was quite a surprise. Up until then, he had never met River and Brooke. Jeremy and his groomsmen all had their tuxes fitted and ordered, and my bridesmaids were happy with their beautiful, flowy, fuchsia-coloured dresses. I, on the other hand, was still waiting for my dress and getting anxious. I called the seamstress a few days before the wedding and found out that she had her dates mixed up and hadn't worked on it at all, which made her rushed when she was doing the final touches on the dress. When I tried it on the night before the wedding, it was a little bit too big, but it would have to do.

On the morning of the wedding, the bridesmaids and I got ready at the house. We did our hair and makeup while treating ourselves with expensive champagne and orange juice. Jeremy and his groomsmen were at the hotel room that was reserved for us after the wedding. Jeremy handed out pocket knives to his groomsmen while they pounded back the whiskey.

It was a beautiful, sunny day, not a cloud in the sky. My dad was making up for lost time getting to know his grandkids, and he was happy to be a part of my big day. He had his old, clunky camera hanging around his neck and was taking a million pictures with it.

Catherine & her daughter on the day of her wedding

They would never be developed though, because the whole time he had forgotten to put a roll of film in it.

My bridesmaids and I stood on the edge of the patio and had our pictures taken professionally, with a beautiful view of the lake in the background. We must have stirred the sleeping hornets underneath the patio with our commotion, because they started buzzing around us as we screamed, terrified they'd sting us up our dresses. My dad, the hero, took it upon himself to take care of it. Looking back, I should have listened to the signs.

My grandparents never did make it to the wedding. My grandma was bedridden by that time and unable to leave the house. There was such commotion on the day of the wedding that I didn't stop in to visit. I had the full intention of stopping in to visit in my dress, but intentions mean nothing if you don't go through with them. The fact that I was so selfish still breaks my heart to this day. I have never been more thoughtless.

While everyone except the two most important people in

my life was waiting outside of the teepee for me to walk down the aisle, I realized that I had forgotten the wedding papers back at the house. My maid of honour Kristen's husband had to drive back into town to get them. The guests waited in the hot, blistering sun, listening to my musician friend play his solo pieces on guitar, a beautiful mix of techno and Spanish flair. After a couple of hours waiting, I was certain some of the guests were probably thinking that one of us had gotten cold feet. Once the papers arrived, I started my walk down the aisle, arm in arm with my estranged father and led by my beautiful daughter throwing pink flower petals in our path. I focused on the future of our family and tried to see past the negatives. I had high hopes that our marriage would be a new beginning for us.

Jeremy stood under the homemade gate, decorated in twine and flowers, that one of my bridesmaids had made for us. As I walked barefoot on the white aisle runner that led to Jeremy, I could tell that he had had a few drinks, but I was more focused on his hairdo. I wondered why he had chosen to style his hair like a porcupine. His hair was salt and pepper to begin with — he hadn't bothered colouring it black for this occasion — and he had slicked it back with a comb and some gel, leaving it looking like it had a life of its own.

We said our nuptials and signed the papers. By then, everyone was anxious to get out of the hot sun and get the party started, so we made our way back to the reception hall in town. The plan was for the wedding party to enter the reception dancing to an upbeat song, but the DJ got the request wrong and played "The Hockey Song," to Jeremy's delight.

The reception was set up beautifully, with large, stargazer flowers everywhere and handmade, candlelit centrepieces. The food was great, and the cake was decorated exactly how I envisioned it. When it was time to cut the cake, link arms and graciously feed it to each other, I mushed a piece of cake onto Jeremy's face instead and he got me back twofold. River even got some on himself. It was picture perfect.

Everything was going smoothly, until my dress fell apart at the seams while the groomsmen at the party twirled me repeatedly during the tune, "I Knew the Bride (When She Used to Rock and Roll)." I tried telling them to stop spinning me, but they couldn't hear me and just kept spinning me faster and faster until my aunt Clara noticed and came to my rescue. My dress had slipped down to my bra and the zipper was broken in the back. If she hadn't gotten to me when she did, my dress would have been down to my ankles.

One girl showed up as a date of one of the guests and, while everyone was up dancing, she bumped into me and spilt her drink down the front of my dress. I ran to the washroom and my bridesmaids blotted it dry, cursing at how she must have done it on purpose. Thankfully, it was white wine and wasn't very noticeable. By the end of the night, my dress was a mess and pieces of my pinned-back updo were hanging down around my face. Brooke was fast asleep in my dad's arms and River was jigging up a storm in his little suspenders for the guests and collecting money just for being cute.

I was in and out of the back door of the reception hall, sneaking a smoke with the other smokers. By the end of the night, I had had a few too many drinks in me, and I always craved a cigarette when tipsy. Out of nowhere, one of the guests started fighting with one of my bridesmaids. The fight was broken up, but not before my dad got punched in the face trying to save me from getting hit in the crossfire. We all went back inside and forgot about the fight, dancing the night away until my bridesmaid decided to go for round two. From across the dance floor, she stormed up to the same girl to serve her a strong uppercut to the chin, taking her down to the ground.

She showed up to the gift opening the next morning looking like a platypus with a fat lip.

Jeremy and I went back to our hotel room together after the reception. The hotel was our mini-getaway from the kids, a substitute for our honeymoon, since we couldn't afford to go on one. When we got woke up the next morning, it was like any other day except we were bound together forever. Or so we thought.

❧

DURING THE WEDDING PLANNING, I hardly recognized how old and feeble my grandparents were getting. I barely made time to talk to my grandma on the phone. I admit I could have made more of an effort, and for that I have no excuse. My biggest regret is that I didn't spend enough time visiting with my grandparents in their last days. Those precious hours that I got to spend with them can never be replaced, and the time that I didn't spend with them will always be wasted time.

It is so important to spend time visiting with family and friends. In our busy lives, we hardly visit anymore. No matter how busy we are, we should make time in our schedules for our families. When I did visit my grandma after not seeing her for some time, I knew she was not doing well. She had lost so much weight. My aunt Loretta took care of her, for the most part, but she was still lonesome and hardly had any visitors.

My grandma was in a lot of pain from her arthritis and wasn't sewing anymore. She had a hard time getting around and mostly lay down because she didn't have much energy. Just days after the wedding, she was in a bad state and we had to bring her to the hospital. She was in and out of consciousness. Our family took turns being there for her overnight in the hospital. She would talk in her sleep and have full conversations with people in her dreams. One night, I saw her sit up in her hospital bed, in agony, in the middle of the night. With her eyes closed, she called out for her favourite brother, who had died a few years before. She often talked about her brother and missed him.

My grandma's will to survive was strong, though, and she wasn't ready to let go. I made the mistake of telling her that she was old one day in the grocery store parking lot. I said, "Grandma, you can wait in the car if you want." I figured it might be too hard for her to get around in the grocery store, and I was just grabbing a few things in a hurry. She got mad at me and said, "What do you mean? I'm still young!" I didn't make that mistake twice. Her mind was young and sharp, but her body was letting her down.

She was released from the hospital a few days later, and our family had to pull ourselves together to look after her, because by that point she was unable to do most things by herself and needed full-time assistance. Coming from a family where she was the thread that held everyone together, it was very hard for us to keep it together for her. We just couldn't seem to organize ourselves and take care of her the way she deserved to be cared for during her last days.

A few weeks later I brought her to the emergency room because she was not well. She was malnourished and dehydrated. She had no appetite and was hardly able to move. I told her that I would be back later; I was busy with the kids and had a few things to do, and I assumed that my aunt would go and be with her in the hospital. As I was leaving the room I turned and waved at her, and a feeling came over me that I couldn't describe. I should have known right then and there that it would be the last time that I would get to visit with her.

Later that evening, I called the hospital and the nurse on the other line sounded relieved. "Thank God you called.

We've been trying to get a hold of a family member," she said. She had been trying to get a hold of my aunt, my grandma's next of kin on her medical chart, but she had been getting a busy signal for hours. My grandma had taken a turn for the worse. No one had been at the hospital by my grandma's side for the entire day. The nurse said that someone needed to get down there right away, because she had had a stroke and was unresponsive.

I rushed to the hospital, picking my aunt up on the way. When we got to the emergency room, my grandma looked like she was sleeping. She was in the same emergency room that I left her in earlier that day. We sat by her side for hours, praying and talking to her. It was only a matter of time until she would let go and meet with the loved ones that had gone before her. I only hope that she heard our last goodbyes and knew how much we loved her.

Our family gathered together for the next three days and prepared her funeral. As is tradition in our culture, we made her a homemade white casket and my uncle made her a cross. We cried and laughed together and told stories of what a remarkable person she was. It was hard to say goodbye to such a wonderful, kind, strong woman who had served others her entire life. She was my mother. Like the delicate glass beads she strung together on the sinew of our moccasins, she was what held our family together. Without her, we were lost.

❧

THEY SAY THAT WHEN YOU truly love someone you can't live without them. My papa stayed at my grandma's house after she died and, a week to the day, he joined her. He couldn't live without her. My grandparents showed me what true, genuine love is. Their love persevered through the hard times, and they never gave up.

Despite his tough demeanor, I think my papa died from a broken heart. Our family gathered around him in the hospital room, where he fought to live. My papa was the strongest person I know, and for him to let go of life gracefully would not be his style. As he lay in his hospital bed he put his arm up in front of his face like he was shielding his eyes, almost like he was being blinded by a bright light. He did this repeatedly and said, "Mom, mom," the same way my grandma was calling out to her brother the night that I stayed by her side in the hospital. They saw something on the other side, in the spirit world, that we couldn't see.

I believe that when someone is close to death, they are in between worlds. That explains why my grandma was reaching out to her late brother the night that I stayed by her side in the hospital. I think that my grandma came for my papa; it was the only way that he would have let go.

Things were different after they passed on. Our family was lost. No one knew what to do. I had lost the only parents I knew, the best parents, in such a short amount of time with no chance to say goodbye. It's so true that you don't know what you have until it's gone. I wish I could go back and sit with my grandma while she played solitaire at the kitchen table, or watch her braid six pieces of string at a time off the fridge door handle for a pair of mitts or mould a pair of moosehide moccasins with her teeth. What I wouldn't give to visit with her again and listen to her tell me stories of her childhood for hours while I helped her roll up endless bundles of yarn.

I wish that I had more time with my papa. I used to cringe when he would start on one of his rants, complaining about the world with his perfectly combed-over hair, which he styled the same way every morning with a jar of shiny brylle cream, muttering something about the "kids these days" out the side of his mouth. He had the demeanour of Clint Eastwood in one of the old cowboy-and-Indian shows that he loved to watch.

Shortly after my papa died, our family was going through pictures of him, trying to find one to use for his funeral pamphlet. They were scattered across my kitchen table when the ceiling lights started to flicker. When he was alive, he used to joke that he was going to play tricks on us when he was gone. Somehow, I knew it was him, so I wasn't afraid.

I heard a knock at the back door of the house the night before his funeral, and I went to the door to see who could be out there so late. I got up and peered through the window, but no one was there. I'm positive that it was my papa. It was the same time that he would come home through the back door after visiting my grandma every night. Maybe he didn't know that he had gone to the other side yet and just wanted to get some rest. Maybe he came to say goodbye before his body was laid to rest.

❧

MY MARRIAGE LASTED SIX MONTHS. I didn't want to be one of those housewives that stayed in an unhappy relationship, pretending everything was okay just because I wanted to have a family and a home that looked good from the outside but was broken on the inside. I didn't want to keep pretending that we were happy anymore.

Our relationship was abusive. Jeremy didn't respect me, and I knew River would stop respecting me too; maybe he would even treat me like his dad did when he grew up if he continued to witness the way I was treated. I needed to do something, anything, but my fear kept holding me back, telling me that we had too much invested in our relationship for me to just up and leave. The house, my business, the kids. I knew that I didn't want to live in the house without Jeremy. It felt wrong living in the home that Jeremy grew up in without him. So, once again, I started exploring education as an option.

I wouldn't be able to get by on the spa alone without a second income, and I definitely wouldn't be able to find a better-paying job because I didn't have a post-secondary education. My only ticket out was going back to school. At least this time I had a certificate to get me started. There was a beautiful school down south that I wanted to attend, and I put a picture of it on my fridge and envisioned myself going to that school one day with my books in hand. I started to look at my life as a mirror that attracted what I saw in my mind and my heart, as if everything I wanted would come to me at the exact time I needed it to, if I just believed enough in the possibility of miracles. I changed my thinking from negative to positive. I started being thankful for everything, despite my shortcomings, and incredible things did start happening. It's amazing what a bit of grit and gratitude can accomplish.

Chapter 11

HAD MY MIND SET THAT I WAS going to be the first person in my family to get a degree. There was no reason for me to stay in Yellowknife anymore. My grandparents were gone, and I felt that I had lost my connection to the North. There was nothing holding me back, and I knew they would have wanted me to be happy more than anything.

With the kids and I leaving town, it gave Jeremy an easy way out of having to be a father. If we didn't live in the same province as him, then he could just feign innocence in not having to visit his kids because they were too far away. The kids were going to miss him, but I knew in time they would understand why I did the things I did.

I sold everything. I left my comfortable home and nice things. My house was full of beautiful furniture and paintings that I had collected over the years, but I've come to realize that things are exactly that — just things. We don't take things with us when we leave this world. We only take with us what we have in our hearts. We all enter this world with nothing but love and, if we are fortunate, that is how we leave it. So, I started to look at material things in that way. I was starting a new chapter in life and needed to purge all of the things that I didn't need anymore. I kept the things that I treasured the most in storage — mostly photos and keepsakes that my grandma made for me — and fit the things I absolutely needed into my little car.

The last time I dreamt of the house, I was in the basement and there was a man standing in the corner in the dark, staring at me. I couldn't make out his face. That's when I knew that I wanted more out of life than to be living in an unhappy home. As grateful as I was for the roof over my head, I still needed to live my destiny and follow my purpose in life. And being with Jeremy was not it.

The kids ended up staying behind for a few weeks with Jeremy's mom, while I went ahead to get us set up in our new home down south on Vancouver Island. On my stop in Edmonton, I picked up a friend and we turned my move into a girls' road trip. It was a blast, but when we reached the mountains I was petrified. I had driven on the highway before but never in the mountains. The grandiose peaks and valleys twisted and turned, and the roads were slippery because of the sleet and snow that fell in spades. All I could imagine was flying off the side of a cliff as I carefully drove, grasping the steering wheel until my hands hurt, trying to see past the windshield wipers and the fog. I was driving super slow, trying to take my time going down each mountain, but there were big semi-trucks behind me forcing me to drive faster.

This was not the first long road trip where I was at the wheel. When Brooke was a baby, I had the brilliant idea of driving to Edmonton for the weekend with my mom and the kids. Brooke cried the entire time, and we tried everything to soothe her. We sang nursery rhymes over and over to calm her down, but nothing worked. I was so distracted by her crying that I took the wrong exit and we got lost for hours. By the end of the trip I was practically banging my head against the steering wheel, dreading the long trip home.

This road trip was different. Instead of having to listen to Brooke's holler, I was afraid of dying. When we got out of the mountains and back on level ground, we were making some good speed. We saw something lying in the middle of the road up ahead, but we couldn't make out what it was. When we got closer, we realized it was a dead deer. I had to make a quick decision. If I slammed on the breaks, I would have caused a pile up, so I had to choose: yank the wheel and slam the car into the side of the semi-truck in my right lane, hit the ditch on my left or brace for impact and drive over the carcass. We braced for impact and ran over the dead deer. It was like hitting a large speed bump and the car went flying. We landed safely, glad to be alive. Before I knew it, I had reached my destination.

❧

THE KIDS WOULD BE ARRIVING in a few short days and I had brought our dog Rocky on the road with us. I had to sneak him into the hotel room because there were no pets allowed. Rocky and River had a hard time sleeping without each other and, without River, Rocky was heartbroken. He was so heartbroken that he ran away just hours before the kids arrived. It was an awful way to start the new chapter of our lives. When I picked the kids up at the airport, I didn't know how to break the news to them. I said, "Rocky missed you guys so much that he must have gone on a long walk to look for you and got turned around. I'm sure he'll find his way back to his new home."

Rocky was missing for almost two days. We called the pound, put ads out and filed a missing pet report, but nothing. Then the next evening we got a call from a lady that said she had found him scrounging for food on the side of the road. We were so relieved to have Rocky back. We couldn't have started the new chapter of our lives without him.

Rocky was a special dog. He came into our lives when River and I were living in the city during my days in college. I figured we needed some furry company. I saw an ad in the paper for cheap puppies and went to check it out one night while River was sleeping in the back seat of the car. When I walked into the house, there was a large litter of puppies running around in the kitchen. The owner's kids were playing with them and naming them. I wasn't sure which one to pick until a little girl grabbed the runt of the litter, held him out to me and said, "Here, this one's name is Rocky." And, just like that, he was ours. I couldn't even look at any of the other puppies; it was like he chose me. When we got home that night, I carried River to his bed and put Rocky beside him so he would wake up to a surprise puppy. River and Rocky have been best friends ever since.

Rocky has quite the sense of direction. One night while I was gardening outside, I forgot that I had Rocky with me. I went to bed and locked the door, leaving him outside. Rocky walked all the way up the big hill, through downtown, took a left off Main Street and barked at my grandma's door at three in the morning.

Rocky can roll over and knows how to work for a treat. He can belt out a howl and sing to his favourite songs. He is also a great hunter. One day, I let him roam around the backyard and he came back home with a dead ptarmigan and placed it on my doorstep as a gift. I was so impressed that I cleaned it up and put it in my freezer to be used one day for a good fry. With Rocky found, we moved into our new place and it was almost too good to be true.

❧

OUR NEW HOME WAS FLAWLESS. The small patch of grass in the front yard was a vibrant green and seamlessly manicured. Every row house looked the same, except for the odd house with different coloured trim and flowers. The neighbours were friendly and welcoming. I was the only single Indigenous mother that could be seen for miles, and my neighbours often asked me how I was getting by. The rent was very high, and money was tight, but I tried not to worry about it. I hadn't packed up our lives and come all that way to be defeated. We were going to make it, somehow.

Victoria was beautiful. I had never seen anything like it in all my life. It was a Canadian paradise. Being near the ocean was soothing for my soul, and I would often sit on the beach on a piece of driftwood and just stare out into the beautiful blue abyss whenever I had the chance.

The kids and I were outside as much as possible. Hiking, swimming, camping and exploring. There is no winter in Victoria. The first year we were there, it snowed one day, but melted the next. The kids built a sad-looking snowman that was half dirt and half snow.

My first day of school was a dream come true. I walked, books in hand, down the hill to the school and it looked exactly like the picture that I placed on my fridge a year before; even the weather that day was the same as in the picture. I was proud of myself for how far I had come. I was an official university student. I knew how lucky I was to be in this position, since I didn't graduate from high school. I had made it, despite the odds. Now it was all about focusing and making sure I did the hard work that came along with the prestige.

The next two years were going to be tough, but I was in a beautiful place and I had my little family with me and that was all I needed. I was ready to accomplish my goal of getting a degree and making my family proud. I could only imagine my grandparents looking down on me from heaven, beaming with pride. I finally proved to my papa that he was right all along: I truly was in a "high class" and ready to mingle with the rest of them. I soon found out that I was one of the only Indigenous people in the class and made fast friends with the one other Indigenous woman from the North.

Before that day, I always thought that the highly educated people were smarter than me. In fact, they weren't any smarter. They just appeared to be, because they had privilege, and with privilege comes a sense of confidence. When I saw people that seemed to have it all, I didn't understand why I couldn't be like them. But privilege was not something I would ever know. Most of my classmates came from well-rounded beginnings. Then there was me. I had to go around a time or two before I made it to where I was. In a sense, I had to claw my way to the top. I am glad that I didn't have it easy, because success means a lot more to me than it does to the people who have everything at their disposal. I did not have my path paved for me from the start, but at the end of the day what mattered was that education gave me the confidence I needed to stand at the same level as those who I thought, all my life, were better than me. I may not have come from the same upbringing or the same race, but I now had the same chance in life. Whenever I felt insecure, I reminded myself that my classmates and I were all in this together, and no one was better than anyone else even though some of my classmates may not have seen things that way. I often had to utilize the school's food bank and was embarrassed to ask for the key to the storage room where the administration kept the dry food. I hoped that none of my classmates would see me. Most of them had probably never experienced the humiliating feeling of not being able to afford food, and I didn't want them to pity me.

I got a part-time job working as a waitress at a pub near our house during my time off from school. I had very little waitressing experience. When I had turned bar age, I had a brief stint as a waitress in a local pub. I was the worst waitress, hands down. I would get drink orders mixed up all the time, even if I wrote them down. I couldn't remember who had what, a tall vodka with two ice cubes and a splash of lemon or a double rye on the rocks. The bar would get so packed on the weekends that I had to learn how to balance my tray above the crowd and somehow squeeze my way through a bunch of rowdy customers without spilling it. I spilled all the time and one time I accidentally spilled the entire tray on this poor fellow who was standing in the wrong place at the wrong time.

My waitressing gig at this pub was less intense, but I still managed to mess up the food orders. My boss starting to give me dirty looks when I got the orders mixed up and the kitchen staff would yell at me when I sent food back. I was often sent into the kitchen to do the dishes in the back instead of dealing with unhappy customers.

Some of the customers were so rude, and I had no patience for it. One lady tried to give me a few pennies as a tip and I said, "It's okay, keep it." Another time a man was so picky, he sent his food back three times. When he asked for ketchup with a snotty attitude, I grabbed the ketchup and dropped it onto the table in front of him and it splashed all over his nice clean white shirt. I apologized but couldn't help but think that he might have deserved it.

My customers must have complained about the poor service, because I eventually got fired. I didn't disagree with my boss's decision to fire me, but she did it in such a ruthless manner, right before Christmas. She said, "I'm sorry, Catherine but you're just costing me too much money. You're constantly getting your orders mixed up." I had never been fired before. I wanted to defend myself, but instead I didn't say a word and walked out feeling sheepish. At least now I know that my calling is not waitressing. It's a tough job and, since then, I have had the utmost respect for people working in the hospitality industry.

I took a job as a security guard shortly after that; since I was taking my degree in justice, I thought it would make sense to start working in a somewhat related field. I was posted in various locations around the city. My least favourite posting was the liquor store, where I had to stand on guard in my uncomfortable uniform for hours, feeling like a British guard. I would take my time wandering around the store, becoming very familiar with each type of wine and spirits. I did the rounds outside of the store on the hour to pass the time, but mostly I would just stand until my feet felt like they were melting into the floor beneath me. I tried to imagine that I was a strong tree with my feet rooted firmly in the ground, but it just made my feet ache even more.

While working the rounds in a downtown building one day, I got chased in the back alley by a homeless person on a bicycle, which left me winded. The last straw was when my employer wanted me to do the rounds in an underground parking lot at six in the morning, without a weapon. I wasn't about to take a chance of getting murdered in an underground parking garage in the city, so I turned in my uniform and that was the end of my security guard days.

❧

JEREMY CAME TO VISIT ME and the kids halfway through our first year on the island and brought his unwanted turmoil with him. His "visit" turned into him permeating himself back into our lives. I know he didn't mean to be the way he was, but he travelled all the way to see us only to be a thorn in my side once again.

I was going to the gym daily at the school, working out on

my own and doing some circuit training classes. I was preparing to take a physical test to become a corrections officer and needed to be in the best shape possible. I passed the physical test but didn't want the job after all, because I chickened out when I took a tour of the prison. Something about having to be confined in a small space all day with convicted felons didn't sit well with me, and if I couldn't make it as a security guard than the odds were that I couldn't make it in a maximum-security prison, either.

Jeremy bought himself an electric scooter because he did not have his licence and had to have some way of commuting to the warehouse job he got on the other side of town. At first he purchased an electric bicycle from a local outdoor flea market, but it stopped working days later, so he upgraded to a used electric scooter that ran off a battery pack and had to be plugged into an outlet to charge.

As he set off to work, he looked so ridiculous and oversized on his silver scooter with the Superman sticker slapped on the front. He travelled on the sidewalk at five kilometres an hour, inching his way to work before the crack of dawn. His scooter had just enough juice in it to get to work, and he had to charge it up during the day to make his trip back home.

One weekend, Jeremy decided it would be fun to give scooter rides to the neighbourhood kids while I was out for the day. Jeremy was such a big kid at heart and never knew when to draw the line. He was riding recklessly around the block with Brooke on the back and crashed into the neighbour's door. Shortly afterward, he crashed again after running over the neighbour's pug. The poor pug skidded on its belly for a few feet until Jeremy realized what he had done. When I got home, he was in a heap on the ground next to the broken scooter, muttering something about wanting to go back to the North where he could go fishing — something that he hardly ever did to begin with. The neighbour rushed the poor little pug to the vet. The pug survived, but it had severe road rash and had to wear a cone for the next couple of weeks. I'm not sure if it was the pug that did it — maybe it was the mix of chaos and years of going through the same ups and downs — but whatever it was, my mind was finally made up. I was done.

I'll never forget the day that the kids and I drove their dad to the airport to catch his flight back to Yellowknife. We all knew that this was finally it. The last episode in the saga of Catherine and Jeremy. We had failed at every attempt to be together, and it was time to stop trying. I let one tear roll down the side of my face. I didn't wipe it away in case he saw me crying, so I just let it dry up on my chin. The kids were silent. On any normal car ride, they would be fighting and screaming in the back seat, but they knew well enough to behave on this ride. The kids hugged him as he waited in line at the airport to check in. They didn't shed a tear. If it were me leaving, they would be crying, devastated. I breathed a sigh of relief when we drove out of the airport parking lot. I realized that, all this time, I had been holding my breath. And I could finally breathe again. I knew the kids and I would be okay; as sad as it was, they were used to having their dad leave sporadically. It didn't take us long to bounce back into our routine, without looking back.

❧

I GRADUATED FROM MY Bachelor of Arts in Justice that fall and was surprised with how easy the workload had been. I wasn't ready to stop living on the island or learning, so I signed up for a master's program at the university.

When I told my mom about my educational pursuits, she was happy for me, but she didn't understand why I was still in school after I had already achieved my goal of getting a degree. I tried to explain to her what a master's degree was, but I gave up trying to get her to understand why I was still in school. I knew she was proud of me. She just didn't exactly know how to go about showing it.

I got a job across town working in a small salon. I just couldn't get away from the spa practice, but it served me well and was something I could always fall back on if need be. We moved into a small apartment around the corner from the salon, trending with unique boutiques, outdoor food markets and live music on every street corner. I loved being submersed in the charm and the culture of the island.

A little, one-bedroom apartment was all that we could afford, since I was only working part time at the salon, and it reminded me of when I lived with my grandma. River and Brooke shared the only bedroom in our cramped apartment, and my bed was set up in the dining area under a brass chandelier. Our kitchen couldn't fit more than one person at a time. It wasn't the ideal situation, but we were happy and healthy and that was all that mattered.

I became friends with the girls at the spa. I was content, for the most part, but I was still feeling a bit lonely. One of the girls at the spa must have sensed it and said, "You know, Catherine, you should really put myself out there more." A year had gone by since Jeremy left, and it was the longest we had ever been apart. She told me that I should try online dating. I had never thought of it because I was of the opinion that online dating was a sign of desperation, so I was reluctant to sign myself up. But my friend insisted that I would find someone nice and I had nothing to lose.

I set up a profile and found I couldn't keep up with the amount of people on there. It was a daunting task to rifle through the messages and profiles. I was just a drop in the bucket of thousands of lonely people looking for love, or something like it anyway. I connected with someone, and we seemed to hit it off without talking or meeting in person. The concept of blind dating was so out of my comfort zone that, the night that I was supposed to meet him, I stood him up. I wasn't used to having to put myself out there. I needed to learn how to let down my guard, but when he came to pick me up, I wasn't at our meeting spot. He didn't give up so easily on me, though, and on the next try he came to my house to pick me up, so I couldn't back out of it. It was raining hard that day and there was thunder and lightning, something that rarely occurred on the island, so I took it as a good sign.

Trevor was a tall, blonde blue-eyed island boy. He came from a large, close-knit, European family. He lived with his brother in a little brick house with a nice backyard, where they played badminton all year long. His place wasn't too far from mine and, although their house was crumbling, they both owned nice expensive sports cars. When I met Trevor, the first thing that came to mind was that he lied on his profile about being a non-smoker, but it didn't bother me too much.

After dinner, we went for a nice drive around town. He showed me the city from his point of view; having grown up on the island his entire life, he knew all the great spots that only locals would know about. We stopped at a beautiful look-out point with a perfect view of the ocean and stepped out into the rain. We sat on a bench and he leaned over and kissed me under the lightning that filled the sky, and I finally had my romance. I wondered if this is where he took all his dates. He was so handsome; I was almost certain he was a player and that I would get my heart broken, but I was filled with butterflies. I had not had a guy kiss me like that since as far as I can remember. Jeremy had never kissed me with that kind of passion.

Trevor was sweet, yet he still had a bad boy image to him

that I took a liking to. I had been with Jeremy for so long that, when Trevor did nice things for me, I would always be taken by surprise. I slowly started understanding that this was what a healthy relationship must look like.

We ended up spending the entire summer together, because Brooke and River were back up north with Jeremy's mother. Jeremy's mother helped me out as often as she could and was one of the only supportive people in my life. She took River and Brooke back to Yellowknife that summer so that I could have a break from the stress of taking care of the kids on my own. Little did I know that I would meet a special someone and focus all my time and attention on him.

Trevor and I fell in love that summer. In the fall, when the kids were back with me, Trevor and I would go for long walks together and sneak away to the beach while they were in school. We would spend our time tanning, walking barefoot in the sand, collecting pieces of driftwood and beach glass. Things seemed perfect, but trouble in paradise slowly started brewing. River didn't like Trevor. No matter how hard Trevor tried, he just couldn't get River to warm up to him. Of course, it was to be expected that River didn't want anyone replacing his dad and I didn't push the issue. But Trevor went to extremes to try to get River to like him and even went as far as renting a boat one summer day to have one-on-one time with River. Being out in the middle of the ocean was Trevor's idea of man-to-man bonding. I look back now and wonder why I ever allowed Trevor to take River out into the middle of the ocean in the first place. Trevor didn't know the first thing about boats, let alone where he was going.

They left in the early morning, and I was pacing the floors by the time evening rolled around. When Trevor finally called me and solemnly said, "Catherine … something bad happened," my heart sank. He said he would tell me when he got to the house. I could only imagine the worst. I wanted to scream. By the time Trevor pulled up to the house, I was already outside on the sidewalk. I watched him pull up with River in the passenger side, and relief went through me like a wave. I hugged River tight while he and Trevor laughed and laughed about how overprotective I was.

I was so mad at Trevor for making me think that something bad happened to River. All I could think was that River went overboard. "What's wrong with you? Why would you joke like that?" I asked. It turned out they had a great time out on the ocean, but it still wasn't enough to win River over. Poor Trevor was sick in bed for a week afterward with vertigo. He told me that, at one point, they ended up way too far out on the ocean and he got so turned around that he didn't know which way the shore was. He knew they were in trouble because the waves were getting bigger and he was surprised that they made it back in one piece without capsizing.

I knew it would take time for Trevor to gain the respect of River but, after a while, I began to get a bit impatient with Trevor because we had been together for almost a year and I wanted to take the next step in the relationship. In my experience, people usually "shack up" after a few months — sometimes weeks — so I didn't think it was a big adjustment moving in together after a year. But he wasn't ready or willing to make changes in his life to include me and the kids in it. He was afraid of the commitment.

I asked that we start making plans to move in together, but he just wouldn't talk about the subject or dodged it whenever I brought it up in conversation. He was happy living with his brother and couldn't see how it would work if the kids and I moved in.

Trevor continued to show me his love and affection by buying me things to try to keep me from straying. He bought me a beautiful crystal bracelet and gave it to me one day in the parking lot of a fancy yacht club restaurant, where we would go and have brunch while he talked about his plan of buying a nice boat someday. I tried the bracelet on, but it didn't fit. It was too small and, as we drove away, he accidently ran over a pigeon. I took it as a sign.

Trevor even went as far as buying me a cat, without telling me. He was driving to my house one day to visit, when I heard something meowing over the phone in the background. I had told him in a side conversation once about how I would love to have a kitten, but I didn't think he would take me seriously. He came over one day with a Siamese cat. Poor River was allergic to it, and the cat had to be brought back to the pet store. Trevor packed the cat up in its little carry-on kennel and walked out of the apartment with his head down, looking like the Cat in the Hat.

After the spa that I was working in shut down because of poor management, I started working in the kitchen at a navy base on the edge of the ocean. My day began at four in the morning, but I didn't complain because finding work was difficult and I had to take what I could get. It paid better than my security guard stint and the spa combined, but even though I was busting my butt going to school and working, I was still not making ends meet. Something needed to give. I was growing tired of having to live in a cramped, one-bedroom apartment and needed to make a move.

Since Trevor wasn't changing his mind about taking the next step in our relationship, I decided to move into a small, two-bedroom basement apartment next to a park in an older part of town, so that the kids and I could have more room. The place was crawling with spiders, and the ceilings were so low that Trevor had to duck to walk around in it. He would hit his head on some of the lower sections of the ceiling from time to time, so when he came to visit we would usually go sit in the park or take his precious dog — his pride and joy — for a walk. I started to wonder if he loved that dog more than me, and I began to resent it. I couldn't believe I was jealous of a dog, but the dog got more attention from Trevor than I did. It got to snuggle with Trevor at night, and I didn't. Trevor and I began to argue a lot. Our stagnant situation was the cause for most of our arguments. I was growing impatient with him. His family was not very keen on him being with me either, and I assumed it had something to do with the fact that I was still technically married and an Indigenous mother of two from way up North.

When I first met his family, they were very accepting of me. They thought that I was Parisian and his dad was happy that his son had finally met a nice girl. He was overly welcoming when I came to visit. Shortly after they found out my circumstances, they stopped extending the invite for me to come to their family dinners. I didn't let that bother me too much, and Trevor played it off like it wasn't a big deal, but I should have known it was the beginning of the end. Once your family doesn't like the person you are dating, it's pretty much game over from then on.

I had to think realistically about my relationship with Trevor and stop thinking with my heart over everything else. I knew that my days in the South were limited because I was soon going to have to start paying back my student loans, and I needed to start thinking seriously about the future. I was especially having a hard time finding a decent-paying job; even with my bachelor's degree, I was considered a dime a dozen. I knew that, if I went back to Yellowknife, I could get a good-paying job and that possibility was always in the back of my mind. The North was calling me home, whether I liked it or not.

When I told Trevor that I was at a crossroads and needed him to make up his mind about the next step in our relationship, I knew that it could either make us or break us. "If we don't move in together soon, I have to go back to Yellowknife," I said. It sounded like a threat, and I really didn't want to move back. I loved our little piece of paradise on the island and didn't want to leave. It would be like admitting defeat, and I have never been a quitter – but the only reason I was staying was Trevor, and it wasn't enough.

This little ultimatum turned out to be perfect timing, or so I thought. Trevor said that he might have found a place for us and brought me to have a look. The home was beautiful. He walked me through the bones of the house and, although it was still under construction, it had all the bells and whistles. It even had a fully equipped basement suite with a kitchen and washroom. It was perfect. A dream come true.

Finally, Trevor and I could start our lives together. When I asked Trevor what his brother was going to do once he moved out, he just assumed I had already known what the plan was. His brother was going to also live in the house with us, so of course I automatically thought that his brother would live in the basement suite. I couldn't have been more wrong. The entire time, his plan was that his brother would live in the top part of the house with him, while the kids and I rented out the basement suite for a cheap price. Essentially, he would be my landlord. I thought he was joking and trying to get a rise out of me. I laughed at him over the phone after he told me and said, "You're kidding, right?" But there was silence on the other end. He couldn't understand why I had a problem with his proposal. He didn't see how degrading it sounded to me. He thought I was being ungrateful. "Why are you always like this?" he asked. I told him that there would be no way that I would rent a basement suite off him while he and his brother lived upstairs as my landlords, only for him to come down and visit me when he felt like it or invite me up when it was ideal for him.

I felt like the toy that he played with whenever it was convenient for him, and he thought he could just put me back in the toy box when he was done. I wasn't going to be his doll anymore. That was the breaking point for me, and I knew what I needed to do. I made the difficult decision to end things with Trevor. He didn't exactly try reconciling with me either, which made my decision that much easier. I was going home.

Chapter 12

I BOOKED THE CHEAPEST FLIGHTS BACK to Yellowknife I could find to fly the kids home while I figured out my plan of action. I had to put my heartbreak aside and focus all my attention on my future, but I was torn about having to say goodbye to the island. I wasn't sure if I was more upset about my breakup with Trevor or my breakup with the island. I thought for sure I would stay there forever, but the North has always been there for me, unyielding, steadfast and strong.

Trevor called when it was too late to change my mind. It always took him a long time to get around to calling me after an argument. "I miss you," he said. He asked me to come over to visit him and talk things over, but I said, "Trevor, I'm gone." He didn't believe me when I told him I was sitting in the airport waiting for my flight. "Sure, sure," he said, until he heard my flight number being called over the loud speakers and I told him, "I have to go." He thought that, all that time, I was just full of empty threats, and my drastic move left him shocked.

After the breakup, I learned that love is a finicky thing. It's tricky and messy and not for everyone. Maybe that's why there are so many lonely people in the world and even those who are with partners can still be lonely. More people need to learn to be happy on their own without feeling the need to be in a relationship or to having to settle, because it only ends up hurting the other person in the end if their intentions aren't true. I truly believe that, if you are content with yourself, love will find you; you don't have to go looking for it and it won't give up on you if you treat it with care and it is reciprocated. If there is one thing I need in this life, it is to be able to completely trust the person I'm with. I've learned that honesty and respect are hard to find in a relationship, but I won't settle for anything less, even if that means I will be alone. I know that no one is perfect, but red flags and warnings signs are there for a reason and, try as you will to deny them, they are relentless and will eventually come to full light — as I have come to know.

I flew back to the island to get my car after dropping the kids off in Yellowknife. Having to drive it all the way back home was not something I was looking forward to, but I had no other choice. My car was so jam packed with stuff that I couldn't see out the back window. My avocado plant was seated in the passenger side; I just couldn't stand to part with it because the kids and I had planted it together and we were proud of how green our thumbs were. Every time I hit a bump on the highway my stuff in the back seat would bounce, including my grandma's heavy cast iron pan that I haphazardly placed behind my seat, which came close to knocking me out a few times.

When I got back to Yellowknife, I rented a small, two-bedroom basement suite. I just couldn't get away from the basement suites, but at least this one was free of spiders and low ceilings. In Yellowknife, it is so hard to find a decent rental and the housing market rents are extremely high. I ended up paying double what I paid on the island, and I could hear the people upstairs talking over dinner because their kitchen was right above our entryway and their voices echoed through the house.

I had the hardest time finding a job when I got back. I was lucky if I even got a call back for an interview. I couldn't understand why the doors weren't opening for me. I went above and beyond, out of my comfort zone, to get an education. I travelled away from home and took out a large loan to pay for my future and the future of my children. I wanted them to have what I didn't have growing up. I wanted to be a strong light in their life — to prove to them that you can do anything you put your mind and heart to if you believe and you are driven — but I still felt like I had failed somehow. I was always told that educated Indigenous northerners were few and far between in the North and that, if I were to get a higher education, I would find a job easily. But it was not so. I felt like everything I had striven for was in vain. It was all a joke. A false advertisement that I had bought into. There were no awards, no pats on the back or kind words of recognition that I thought I would receive. I didn't even have a chance to celebrate with my classmates at my convocation because the awards ceremony was a year after my graduation date and, by then, I was back in Yellowknife barely able to pay my rent and couldn't afford to travel. So, things didn't exactly play out like I had dreamed. There was no happily ever after. No finish line. As exhausted as I was, though, I had to keep going.

I finally got a job, two months after returning to Yellowknife after much persistence. Even though it was an entry-level job that was below my educational experience, I was relieved to be working and making money. After two years in the basement suite, I decided to move out and into a townhome. It seemed like the right thing to do because there would be more room for us. I should have known that it was a bad idea. I didn't budget properly, and the townhome was even more expensive. I realized quickly that I was house broke. After one month, I made the very difficult decision to move in with my mom and stepdad with a plan to save up enough money to buy a house.

✍

FOR THE NEXT THREE MONTHS, the kids and I lived in the back of my mom's two-bedroom trailer with our entire lives, including our pets, stuffed into one small bedroom where there was nothing more than a foot of old carpet to maneuver on.

We hid in the back room of the trailer and kept as quiet as we could every time one of the landlords came over, because if they found out we were staying there, they might have hiked up the rent. We were overcrowded, but it was our only option for getting ahead.

My plan was less than ideal, but we sucked it up and lived like sardines for the next three months so I could save most of my earnings to put toward a down payment on a house. The kids and I were used to living in close quarters and didn't mind it. Besides, knowing that we were doing this with an end goal in sight made things even easier. When an affordable place became available on the market, I had to jump at the opportunity. At that time, I didn't have enough money saved up to buy the house I really wanted, but I was still able to save up enough money to make a down payment on a trailer and that was going to have to do.

At first, I felt too proud to even consider living in a trailer, but my humble beginnings reminded me that having material things was not important. I recalled my years growing up and reminded myself that I had come such a long way from where I started, and being a homeowner, even if it was just a trailer, was an exceptional accomplishment. After living in one-bedroom apartments and low-cost housing most of my life, having a place to truly call home was a dream come true. I've moved around so much in my life, but the one thing I know for sure is that a home is where your loved ones are and where you can find comfort, happiness, peace and love. A home is not a large, immaculate, expensive, empty house with fancy furniture. Home is what you make it, and when River, Brooke and I moved into our little trailer, it suited us just fine. As long as we were healthy, happy, safe and loved then we could conquer anything.

As a new homeowner, I soon realized that, when something was broken, I had to fix it. I couldn't call the landlord and expect them to come fix the furnace and repair the leaky roof; it was all on me. If I had it my way, I would live the way my grandmother did, off the grid, immersed in nature and living by our own rules, our own Indigenous laws and governance, our own ways of being. I know that it is coming. A full circle is forming.

When I look back on how far I have come, I feel that I can cope with life's everyday difficulties with a little more grace. I have my good and bad days, but I continue to make a constant effort and push myself to be better. By pushing myself and going after my dreams, I have changed the course of my life, and it all started with getting an education.

I learned along the way that success is not about how smart you are or how much you can attain. Many people think that success comes after they accomplish something that they have striven toward, but it is far from it. The constant pursuit of achievement never ends. Once you've surpassed your own personal expectations, you make new ones so that there is constant growth. I take risks and go after my aspirations, and that's what makes all the difference. It took me over a decade to get to the point where I feel I can finally look back and see that I have come a long way.

From the moment I started on my journey toward a higher education and a better life for myself and my children, it hasn't been easy. I didn't realize until later on that I needed to learn how to be happy while going after my dreams, because that is what matters. Enjoying the winding road while you are on it, acknowledging the time it will take to reach your destination, forgiving yourself when you fail and not giving up when times get tough are what is important. Knowing that there are amazing feats to look forward to and new horizons to reach is what keeps me going. Most importantly, I have learned that there is a lot of work to be done to ensure that Indigenous people in this country are treated with respect and dignity and that is what gets me up in the morning. I fight every day in big and small ways to break down the systems that have blinded us and confined us. I feel that I am fighting the good fight, the only fight left worth fighting.

I faced many barriers along my journey and they are mostly because I am an Indigenous single mother trying to make a life for myself and my children in a world that still does not accept us. I used to try to fit into the mould of modern day society, own a nice home, an expensive car, make and save lots of money. But I was constantly chasing something that would never make me truly happy and it's because I didn't know any better. I used to get jealous when I saw other people that seemed to have it all. Now I know better. Now I know that, my entire life, I had something more powerful than money could ever buy. I carried the Dene values and traditions of my ancestors within me, quietly guiding me on my journey, waiting to be discovered. I am glad I never fit into the mould. Instead of buying into the dream of what I was told my life is supposed to look like, I use my education as a weapon for change. I am now in a position to help generate awareness on the systemic racism against Indigenous people in Canada that still drives our nation, and I am on a mission to empower Indigenous people to gain back their identity. I am starting the conversation about decolonization in my home with my children. I'm trying to instill in them a sense of pride in who they are and where they come from. I want them to speak their language and immerse themselves in their culture. I want them to be respected for who they are. My job as their mother is to try and make the world a little bit safer, a little bit kinder, a more welcoming place for them to live in. To give them the freedom to test the limits, challenge those who tell them they can't and give them the hope and the courage they need to dream up new possibilities.

I hope that, by working toward my goals, it will help my children to see that anything they want to accomplish can happen if they put in the effort. I can only hope that, in the future, my children will be courageous and proud of who they are, unafraid to speak up for themselves and go after their goals.

Sometimes I wonder if I am still lost, but then there are times when I receive signs that I am on the right path, and I hold on to those moments for as long as I can. The last time that I had such a strong message was while I was telling a story about my grandma to a friend of mine, and a woman nearby overheard me. She said, "I know your grandma; I took her sewing class." My grandma taught a sewing class at the local friendship centre every Thursday night when I was a little girl. Instead of taking up sewing, I would draw pictures of my dream home while listening to my grandma and the other women in the class gossip and laugh while she helped them undo their stitches and start all over if they made a mistake. The woman said, "I have something to give you," and the next day she met up with me and brought a pattern of flowers that my grandma had drawn for her to be used to make a pair of moccasins. I instantly recognized my grandma's flowers. She said, "Your grandma gave me this pattern to practise beading, and I never found the time to sew. I've been hanging onto these for almost thirty years." I unfolded the cloth and was instantly taken back to my childhood. I was back at my grandma's kitchen table, listening to her humming while she sewed. I tried to hold back my tears. The woman held my hand and said, "Keep it, it means more to you than me."

When I got home that day, I carefully traced the outline of the flowers that my grandma drew. I knew what I had to do. I gave a copy to my mother and asked her to use the drawing to sew moccasins for her grandchildren, and for the first time in a long time, she picked up a needle and thread and starting beading. The pattern was a gift from my grandma meant to help guide us on the path toward reclaiming our identities.

With me in spirit, my journey is forever guided by my grandmother's wisdom and the gift she gave of an everlasting love, now found in the miraculous splendour of a northern wildflower reminding me to be brave, strong, wild and free.

Epilogue

CATHERINE NOW SERVES IN HER community as a leader. In 2016 she was elected to sit on the Council for her First Nation, where she serves as one of the Council members and holds the portfolio for justice, heritage and housing. Catherine is also the Director of Indigenous Education and Community Development for Dechinta Bush University, a land-based university located in the Northwest Territories that is rooted in Indigenous culture and traditions while providing post-secondary education in the fields of Indigenous governance, colonialism and decolonization. Catherine would have never thought that she would one day become a foster parent after having herself been a foster child; however, she has been fortunate enough to be able to give back and feels blessed to be able to provide stability, love and care in a nurturing home environment for those in need.